A MORE PERFECT UNION

A FISCAL PLAN FOR AMERICA

Stuart Dunn

AuthorHouse™
1663 Liberty Drive
Bloomington, IN 47403
www.authorhouse.com
Phone: 1-800-839-8640

Published by AuthorHouse 05/28/2013

ISBN: 978-1-4817-4060-9 (sc)
ISBN: 978-1-4817-4061-6 (e)

Library of Congress Control Number: 2013906896

"Civilization works only if those who enjoy its benefits are also prepared to pay their share of the costs. Getting rich people to pay their dues is an admirable ambition, but leaders who want to make their countries work better should focus instead on cleaning up their own backyards and reforming their tax systems."

The Economist, February 16th, 2013

"Countries cannot consistently run large deficits; and sustained growth is not possible with hyper inflation. Some level of discipline is required."

Globalization and its Discontents, Joseph E. Stiglitz

Contents

i. Open Letter to the President

President Obama;

Congratulations on your reelection. The 2012 election was about personal freedom; citizenship rights; and concern for the poor, the elderly and the sick. Most of all it was about the federal budget, the national economy, and jobs. Your inaugural speech, in the tradition of Abraham Lincoln and Franklin Roosevelt, defined a vision for America. Your State-of-the-union address on February 12, 2013 was a worthy follow up. It is clear that you recognize the fundamental challenges America faces. But, identifying the problems does not constitute a plan to solve them.

Your reelection was a great political accomplishment, but the job of uniting the country politically is just begun. America is increasingly diverse...racially, ethnically, religiously and even linguistically. The traditional family has been replaced by an array of relationships. We are an aging and demographically changing nation.

Where to start? America is economically challenged, perhaps as we have not been since the Great Depression and Washington has been unable to address the problems. The gap between the ultra-wealthy and the rest of the population threatens not only our economy, but our political equality as well. Unemployment remains high and middle class incomes have stagnated. Many of those who have lost their jobs and found new employment have had to accept reduced income. Public debt has been piling up as we fought two unfunded wars in the Middle East and suffered a profound economic crisis. (While the deficit is expected to fall in FY2013, unless we make significant budgetary changes it will continue into the foreseeable future.) Our active involvement has ended in Iraq and is drawing down in Afghanistan, but world peace remains elusive and the threat of terrorism persists. Global warming is increasing. Bio-medical, computers and technological advancement demand increasing knowledge while our education system is leaving too many behind. These problems cannot be addressed successfully without addressing our national economy and the role of the federal government.

You have been attempting to do this over the opposition of reactionary forces funded by billionaire's and big business' money. Congress has not passed a budget in four years. Congressman Hoyer (D-MD) said "You don't need a budget....We can adopt appropriation bills without a budget." I believe Congress hasn't passed a budget because we have not had a national fiscal plan. It is time to develop one. Unfortunately, although you have touched on a number of areas which should be a part of such a plan, such as raising the minimum wage, you have not proposed an integrated plan. This book does that, and I hope it will be useful to you.

There was widespread rejoicing (and a significant rally on Wall Street) following the last minute deal brokered by Vice-president Joe Biden and Senator Mitch McConnell, to avert the so-called "fiscal cliff" at the beginning of 2013. The two month delay negotiated in activating "sequestration" is over, and we are now encountering these arbitrary budgetary cuts. Just how these cuts will affect the economy is unknown, but investors seem unconcerned. The deal agreed to two months earlier, rather than showing how the right and the left can cooperate in addressing our fiscal problems, illustrates how difficult it is to face the real issues. (For example, it is clear that further tax increases will be necessary, but Senator McConnell says "tax increases are finished".) Undoubtedly, another "compromise" will be reached to keep the government functioning, but, we cannot just continue to avoid the underlying issues. We need a long-term plan, but, what we get are the same worn clichés: we must c**ompromise** (with whom, on what?), the economy needs another (unfunded) **fiscal stimulus,** the problem is (the cost of) the **entitlements,** we **can't balance** the budget by **taxing the wealthy** (Has anyone done the math? Federal revenue as a percent of GDP is below the average for the past 50 years.), **poverty will always be with** us (Why?), **jobs** have permanently **gone overseas** (a reversible trend), we have reached the **end of the American era** (America is still the indispensible nation). It amazes me how so many economists and politicians have nothing to offer except the same clichés, half truths and outright lies. This book offers a different approach.

You have received a great deal of criticism for focusing on health care during your first administration, rather than addressing the economic crisis more generally. I don't agree. Your actions on TARP, the fiscal stimulus, unemployment compensation, and food stamps were critical and contributed to avoiding a disastrous depression. I agree with those who advocated a larger, longer-term fiscal stimulus, but as Secretary of State Hillary Clinton said in her recent appearance before the Senate Foreign Relations Committee "what does it matter now?" We should learn from experience, but, the important question is where do we go from here? I believe that by addressing health care you were addressing the economy as well.

Your focus on health care was correct. Alan Blinder in his book, *After the Music Stopped: The Financial Crisis, the Response and Work Ahead,* concludes: "In the long run, we don't have a European style generalized deficit problem in this country. We have a health care cost problem." Health care is an enormous contributor to America's GDP, about $2.6 trillion, out of an annual total of $15 trillion. If I have learned anything from my own experience it is, "take care of the dollars and the pennies will take care of themselves." (No, I did not get that backwards.) In other words, focus first on the big ticket items. Since health care is the largest national expense, it was, and is, correct to focus on it. But, it must be treated as part of the overall social and economic problems.

Not surprisingly, what you found was a health care system in which 50 million people had no insurance, a system which was in need of expansion rather than contraction and a system which is inefficient and badly overpriced. Congress forced you address health care by extending private health insurance rather than replacing it with single-payer government health insurance. As a result, America got a flawed plan (albeit, better than none), and you were unable to free up private and state health care dollars to invest in stimulating the economy. Currently, the federal government spends about 1/3 of the total money spent each year on health care in this country and it is rapidly growing. The Affordable Care Act will further increase this cost. The built-in savings fail to compensate for the increased government cost. Even worse, it is becoming clear that some states will opt out of expanding Medicaid, and that the insurance companies will, under this act, raise rates to private individuals and employers.

The other two big areas of federal outlay are Social Security and Defense. Despite what right wingers say, Social Security is not part of the problem (However, it can be part of the solution, but not by decreasing or delaying benefits.) It is, and has been, self-supporting. The budget for the Defense Department already has cuts built in which largely reflect the end of our active involvement in Iraq and Afghanistan. In a dangerous world, further cuts must be very carefully made. But, it clear that the budgetary control in the Defense Department is inadequate and waste widespread. These issues must be addressed.

So what should you do? We hear that no economic fix is possible without cutting entitlements. I believe this is the wrong approach. This book calls for single-payer, Medicare-like universal health insurance to be provided by the federal government. Indeed, it is central to the plan. This will cost the federal government more, but will free up about $1.5 trillion each year in private, state and municipal dollars. Not only is it the right thing to do, it would set the stage for significant overall savings in the cost of health care in America and would constitute a huge, and ongoing, economic stimulus package. The American economy is poised for a break- out. This plan could insure that happening.

Since I am also advocating balancing the budget, the money to pay for universal health insurance will have to come from someplace. The places I propose are: increased income taxes (at a net cost increase for the wealthy only), levying some new fees and taxes, and addressing waste, fraud and inefficiency in health care delivery and in government services. (The potential savings in the cost of medical care has been estimated to be as much as $750 billion a year. This saving would make the per capita cost of health care in America more consistent with that of other industrialized countries.) Balancing the budget must go hand-in-hand with increased employment opportunity and the elimination of poverty. To accomplish these objectives, my plan is designed to stimulate the economy, will bring jobs home from overseas, increases the minimum wage, and where necessary, makes the federal government the employer of last resort.

I will not attempt to explain my plan in detail here. For that you have to read the book. As you do so, keep in mind that money spent on health care by other than the federal government: Medicare - payroll taxes by individuals and business and other contributions, parts B, C and D, - Medicaid - state and municipalities costs, business - employee health insurance, and individual - privately purchased insurance and direct cost; together with the other payroll tax contributor, Social Security, are going to be the source for much of the dollars to needed to address other areas of the economy. Under the proposed plan, this money **does not come from cutting benefits,** but by financing entitlements out of progressive income taxes replacing the current regressive payroll taxes. There are many other areas beside entitlements which need to be financed including: economic growth; full employment; infrastructure; mass transit; renewable energy generation, smart distribution, and conservation; education; environmental protection; habitat and species preservation. This plan will ultimately make available funds to finance these critical areas.

A paper by Yale University Professor Jacob Hacker, *Prosperity Economics: Building an Economy for All,* concludes, "There is no trade-off between creating a strong, dynamic economy and fostering a society marked by greater health, broader security, increased equality of opportunity and more broadly distributed growth."[1]

---

1 SEIU Blog, August, 2012

Balancing the budget requires addressing all federal outlays and receipts. Reductions in non-essential government employees, fairness in public retirement programs and improved efficiency in government operation should be priorities. Among receipts to be addressed are: corporate taxes, a new net worth (wealth) tax, fees for the use of federal land and national resources (restoration of the commons), a financial transaction tax, and a carbon tax.

Now that you have won reelection, the Republican members of Congress talk of compromise to address the economic situation. Compromise is an excellent process when the two parties have good will and reasonable positions to start from. But, as in a marriage, sometimes there are fundamental incompatibilities, or even worse, the lack of any real desire to work things out, and you just have to go your own way. So far, the so-called compromises offered by the Republican Right have been unfair, just nibble around the edges of America's economic problems and do nothing to reduce poverty or address wealth inequality. You should start from where you know we ought to be. You should resist change unless it is comprehensive, fair and looks to the future. The plan described in this book does just that.

This plan proposes a budget for FY2015. Why so far out? The answer is three-fold. First, it is recognized that constructing a budget is time-consuming, especially one which calls for such dramatic changes, and requires considerable lead time. Indeed, the budget for FY2014 is already in preparation at the time this book was written (March, 2013). It will take time to convert this plan to a budget. Second, this plan calls for a complete overhaul of the way we finance the federal government. The public must be informed of the reasons for this plan, its provisions and advantages. It likely will require the Congress elected in 2014 to differ significantly from the sitting Congress. I expect it will take Democratic majorities in both Houses of Congress to get this budget approved. That process will take considerable grass-roots political preparation. FY2015 is consistent with a new Congress. Third, the end of America's involvement in Afghanistan will contribute to a balanced the budget. The wars in Iraq and Afghanistan have cost the U.S. dearly in treasure as well as life, averaging one-half billon dollars a day over the last ten years. Although this cost has already come down, the end of our active involvement in Afghanistan offers the opportunity for further reduction in outlays which can contribute to a balanced budget.

It will be difficult to get this plan approved. Right wing politicians will hate it...Congressman Paul Ryan and the Heritage Foundation are still hung up on killing "Obamacare". Wait 'till they see this plan. The wealthy will hate it...after all, who wants to pay more taxes. The financial community will attack the Financial Transaction Tax. The non-profits will hate this plan...it threatens their revenue stream and their tax exempt status. The pharmaceutical industry and the hospitals will hate it...it will cut into their profit and the exorbitant salaries that their top executives are paid. And, of course, the insurance companies will hate it...it will deprive them of hundreds of billions of dollars of income. So expect a lobbying[2] and media blitz. But, I hope this plan will appeal to you.

Make no mistake...**this will be an ideological war...but you now have a mandate to stand firm. "The Republicans are going to keep their focus on cutting entitlement programs and fighting off tax increases."[3]** Now that sequestration has taken effect they offer continuing resolutions, nominally intended to keep the government running, but actually targeting programs like unemployment insurance and aid to the poor. This is the next skirmish of the fiscal war. You must resist these efforts. They will offer a replay of the Ryan/ Romney 2012 budget designed to eliminate the deficit by cutting entitlements while reducing taxes on the wealthy. They will fight all efforts to bring equity to our fiscal program or to reduce the gap between the wealthy and the rest of America. We need a continuing

---

2 According to Steven Brill, in his article in Time Magazine, entitled, *Why Medical Bills Are Killing Us,* the pharmaceutical and health care-products industries, and organizations representing doctors, hospitals, nursing homes, health services and HMOs spent $5.3 billion (1998 - 2012,) four times as much as the defense industry in the same period for lobbying in Washington, D.C.

3 NY Times, March 6, 2013, *From One Budget fight to the Next*

resolution, but it should over-ride the sequestration and revert to the budgetary allocations before March 1, 2013. It should set aside the limits of the debt ceiling. It should extend through the end of FY2014, after which the plan proposed herein (or something like it) should be your objective.

The more resistant the Republicans prove to be, the better your case will be when you take it to the public. The Conservative Political Action Conference (CPAC), at a meeting in March, 2013, vowed to energize the GOP by putting in place "conservative principles". If, as expected, the Republicans continue to stone-wall progressive legislation, the next election must be about getting a Congress elected which will work for the American people, not just the wealthy and well-connected. George Herbert told us, "He who makes a good war makes a good peace." The Democrats need to energize not just their base, but the American people. This plan can accomplish this objective, and in reenergizing of the Democratic Party, can succeed in electing a Congress which will legislate the most fundamental changes in tax and public policy since President Johnson.

Having a plan is an essential first step. Then, we need a plan to enact this plan, and that Mr. President, is largely in your hands. Hold out for this plan, or something comparable, and take your case to the people. Yes, you can leave a significant legacy, but it won't be easy.

With great enthusiasm,
Stuart Dunn

ii. Preface

America's freedom and prosperity rest on a three-legged stool consisting of its democratic institutions, free-enterprise economy, and enlightenment philosophy. Throughout our history, different elements have taken precedence, but eventually the interplay between the three has brought economic growth, expanded social concern and personal freedom. The only thing constant in American history has been change. Bill Moyers defines American exceptionalism as "the capacity to change".

In 1776 the English colonies banded together to fight for their freedom under the Articles of Confederation. Having won the Revolution, it did not take long to recognize that this agreement could not hold the nation together, and a new document, the Constitution, became the law of the land. The preamble to the Constitution says it was established, "**...in order to form a more perfect union**...", and America has been trying to perfect that union ever since. The Constitution established a democratic/republican federal governmental structure and provided protection to commerce. It granted the federal government a limited right of taxation and the power to deal with foreign governments. A Bill of Rights (the first ten amendments) was quickly added to protect the individual rights of the citizens.

"Andrew Jackson's election in 1828 marked a significant change in American social and political thought. Political institutions underwent a profound transformation, and political control was rapidly transferred from an aristocracy of education, position and wealth to the common man."[4] Under Lincoln the issues were preservation of the Union and ending slavery. Eventually, the freed slaves were recognized as full citizens, although up through the 20th Century the battle against segregation and for voter rights continued. (To some degree, that struggle continues today, over voter identification and quality education.) Theodore Roosevelt spoke out against special interests and for equal opportunity. Rugged individualism consistent with a "frontier mentality" was restrained through such actions as broadening Congressional power to collect taxes, labor laws and limits on monopolies. Universal suffrage brought the woman of America into the political process. (Equality in other ways would have to wait for many years as woman entered the workplace and the military. Salary equity is still an issue.)

Franklin Roosevelt assured workers the right to organize and provided jobs for the unemployed through the WPA and the CCC. Under Social Security, the elderly were assured a secure retirement. Roosevelt mobilized the nation to fight totalitarianism and to shake off a depression which threatened the nation with economic chaos.

Lyndon Johnson added Medicare and Medicaid to protect the sick elderly and poor. Immigration was opened to Asians on an equal basis with Europeans after a century of discrimination. Schools were desegregated and Jim Crow laws preventing Black citizens from voting were largely abolished.

Thomas Jefferson wrote, "The tree of liberty must be refreshed from time to time with the blood of patriots and tyrants." This would appear to be another time to refresh it...hopefully not with blood but with commitment and sacrifice. Democracy is not a stationary thing. It must evolve as our societal needs and circumstances change. It is a living organism. However, as we change, we must honor our history and preserve our fundamental beliefs. And, we must respect and defend each other. The founding fathers concluded the Declaration of Independence, "...we mutually pledge to each other our lives, our fortunes, and our sacred honor." Can we do less?

---

4 *A Documentary History of the United States,* by Richard D. Heffner

When the thirteen colonies threw off the yoke of British rule they defined a new way of governing...with the consent of the people. Richard Heffner[5] writes, 'The Declaration [of Independence] expressed certain fundamental precepts: that all men are equally endowed with the self-evident natural rights of life, liberty and the pursuit of happiness, that civil government is merely an instrument to guarantee those rights within the framework of social order, that when government becomes tyrannical the social compact is broken and it is the "right of the people to alter or to abolish it."' To this day America is struggling to live up to these precepts. Questions abound. Is the government tyrannical when it intervenes in "free-enterprise" or is it negligent when it fails to intervene to protect "we the people"? What are our responsibilities to each other? (Does democracy imply a social contract?) What is the proper balance between individual rights and the needs of society, and what do we mean by "the pursuit of happiness"?

Initially the United States was engaged with defining itself, asserting its prerogatives and testing its growing strength. The Monroe Doctrine, manifest destiny, conquest of the West and even economic imperialism marked our relationships with the world. American prosperity, opportunity and freedom served as beacons which attracted immigrants from everywhere. "Give me your tired, your poor, your huddled masses yearning to breath free...," wrote Emma Lazarus; inscribed on the Statue of Liberty for posterity as a symbol of welcome. The population grew from several million to over 300 million as the nation grew from thirteen to fifty states. In the 20th Century America became the bulwark of freedom defending democracy against totalitarianism. Franklin Roosevelt defined at set of universal freedoms, dubbed, the Four Freedoms: "Freedom of speech and expression, freedom of every person to worship in his own way, freedom from want and freedom and from fear." How were these goals to be achieved at home and abroad? What if people in other nations choose to live differently from ourselves, to have different

5 IBID

values, a different culture? What if they rejected these freedoms? What is our obligation to see that these freedoms exist?

President Obama inherited two divisive wars that diminished America's standing in the world and cost America dearly in lives and fortune. Americans have begun to question our role in spreading our values, nation building and intervention in civil strife abroad. America's power to achieve its international objectives and to spread its ideals world-wide has become limited in the 21st Century. Its freedom of action has been constrained by geopolitical realities, by the growing power of the religious ideology and the recognition of our own limitations. And, in America, a profound economic crisis has put additional limits on our ability to act abroad. America is being forced it to pay increasing attention to its own national problems, to the deep divisions which exist within its society. This book is primarily about America's economic condition, dealing with its increasing national debt and its future in a globalized economy. Politics and world issues affect our economic decisions, but, this book addresses policy rather than politics. The continuing international issues including the nuclear threat, global warming/climate change, and the "clash of civilizations" remain to be addressed elsewhere.

The 2012 voting is over and President Obama has won a second term. This election took place against a background of rallies and conventions, social media, biting political satire, and billions of dollars of television commercials blanketing the airwaves. Through it all, the debate on the role of the federal government became the focal point.

The United States has not been this divided since perhaps the Civil War. This is a battle that has been brewing for decades. In 1964 Lyndon Johnson painted Barry Goldwater as a political extremist and won in an historic landslide. Instead of being remembered for his progressive domestic policies, his legacy was seriously damaged by the Viet Nam War. Jimmy Carter, elected in 1976, saw his popularity crushed by the Iranian hostage crisis and economic woes. The election of Ronald Reagan in 1980 saw the beginning of a philosophical revolution – tax cuts and smaller government, aggressive foreign policy, massive military build-up and accumulation of an increasing national debt. George H. W. Bush followed, waging the first Iraq war and witnessing the fall of the Berlin wall. But, the economy foundered and the national debt continued to grow. In 1992 Bill Clinton was elected, campaigning on the saying, "It's the economy, stupid". He presided over the longest peacetime economic expansion in history, and a budget surplus, but we also saw a widening gap between rich and poor. George W. Bush's administration was defined by the 9/11 terrorist attack followed by two Middle Eastern wars, an unwise tax cut and a massive economic crisis.

In 2008 Barack Obama was elected on a platform of hope and change. He was not able to accomplish many of his objectives as the "tea party" emerged to control a Republican House of Representatives. In the recent election, throughout the campaign, the candidates positioned themselves as leaders of two opposing camps on the size of the federal government and the economy. "The real question is not the size of the government, or even its role, but rather whose side the government is on. Has it been bought and sold by the one per cent, or is there still room for the 99 per cent? Or even the 47 per cent? How different will the US look in the next four years? With a divided Congress and citizenry, will partisan gridlock rule, or will the Obama administration, given four more years, alter America's path?"[6]

Not since the 1930s has America faced economic decisions as profound as it faces now. The ability of our economic system to provide full employment is in question. Some call for another financial stimulus, others would set back the gains in social welfare made in the past 80 years to balance the budget. "Many Americans have lost confidence that their institutions are working on behalf of the national good. One poll revealed that 61% of Americans believe the country is on the wrong track."[7] The lower income classes have fallen significantly behind. Some think that capitalism itself is the

6 *Choosing the American President,* Top Documentary Filmslargely

7 *The Next American Economy,* by William J. Holstein

problem, that modern corporations are immune to the interests or the will of the people. While I feel that significant change is required, I agree with those who believe[8] "**some version of the free market is the basis of a free society".** My vision is one of a regulated, competitive, free market economy rather than a laissez-faire one. It is one in which the market serves the people rather than visa versa. It is one in which social justice, equal opportunity, and financial equity serve as the basis of political democracy (one person one vote) and individual freedom. Some will say that my proposals are extreme. Let me paraphrase Barry Goldwater, the father of modern conservatism, and say, **extremism in the defense of the American dream is no vice.** But what is the American dream?

(Todd Gitlin writes[9], "...about the fates of two ideas: that of America as a force for individual freedom, and that of the left as a force for equality. They are the two great, heavily burdened ideas of the Enlightenment. They arose from the same stock, these beliefs in progress and redemption: rival claimants to the heritage of freedom, equality and the rest of the promises of the modern world." America has generally adopted the philosophy of democratic Individualism, Europe, social democracy. Each would appear to have problems in today's world. This book opts or something in between.)

Some have said the American dream consists of economic opportunity, jobs and home ownership. Certainly, this was the dream that attracted many immigrants to this country. To others, the dream consists of political freedom, justice and equality under the law. I believe these are both essential pieces of the definition. The elements too often missing when we talk of the American dream are fraternity, mutual responsibility and concern for all who reside here. Concern for each other has not been the thrust of Americanism. We have been more a nation of individuals, perhaps due to our frontier mentality. Well, we are largely over having frontiers. The next logical step in making this nation "a more perfect union" is to address fairness and

---

8 Harry Jaffa, New York Magaizine, October 22, 2011

9 *Why America is Wracked by Culture Wars,* by Todd Gitlin

mutual concern. Much of this is outside the sphere of this book. It includes: expanded individual rights, integration of our more recent immigrants, voting rights, restructuring our electoral system and quality education for all. But, much is within the province of this book: full employment, the elimination of poverty, growth for the middle-class, universal health care, a secure old age and equity in taxation. The fiscal plan proposed herein addresses these and other issues, and dreams of a better America. As Oscar Hammerstein put it, "You've got to have a dream, if you don't have a dream, how are you going to have a dream come true?"

Part 1. Introduction

A nation's fiscal policy is a reflection of its domestic and international policies. It reflects its values, priorities and dreams. It is a product of its economic fortunes, social structure and political philosophy. Thus, this book, in offering a fiscal plan for America, of necessity addresses the underlying questions of where America is at and where it should be going. In an article in the NY Times, dated March 12, 2013, by Annie Lowrey is headlined," *The Dispute Over a Balanced Budget Is Philosophical as Much as Fiscal."* Of course this is true, but it is also true that that the details of the budget you would like to see enacted are also dependent on your philosophy. It makes a big difference whether you want to balance the budget by cutting spending, particularly on entitlements, or by raising taxes on the wealthy. Congressman Paul Ryan may argue that, "ending deficits would foster a healthier and faster-growing economy," but agreeing with that contention does not imply sharing a political philosophy or agreeing with him on how to achieve that objective. Nor does agreeing with Paul Krugman that we need a continuing fiscal stimulus mean agreement that such a stimulus should be deficit financed.

The United States has always been divided politically. Starting as an agrarian society it soon developed industrially taking advantage of its natural resources and the industrial revolution. During the first Century of its existence America was torn by the question of slavery. To the Southerners, slaves were an economic asset associated primarily with their agrarian society. The rest of the country focused on the inhumanity of slavery. The Civil War was about this economic and social issue which divided the nation. While the war resolved the issues of union and slavery, the struggle for civil rights, educational equality and economic well-being for the Black population continues right up to the present. In many ways, the breach between rural and urban, agrarian and industrial, white and black America still exists. It shows up in our social values, our economic priorities and our politics. More recently, the breach has been widened by immigration and demographics.

To some degree, today's economic issues are a replay of the 1930s with somewhat less intensity, but no less urgency. Problems we thought we had resolved then, and during the 1960s, continue to resurface. The financial crisis of the early 21st Century has revived the issues of the role of government in providing social welfare programs and in regulating the financial sector. The gap between the rich and the poor has widened to levels not seen for almost 100 years. The Economist summed it up as follows: "Modern politics needs to undergo a [progressive] reinvention - to come up with ways of mitigating inequality without hurting economic growth."[10]

And, a new factor, the emergence of the global economy has put American industry and industrial workers under the pressure of intense international competition. Science and technology, exemplified by computer science, technology and bio-medical advances, has made advanced education a virtual necessity to qualify for a decent job, and our education system has been unable to keep up with the need.

What is behind the current economic crisis? First, it's the lack of jobs. While the official unemployment rate has fallen, there is a serious question of just how significant this is. Many who are unemployed have been unemployed for over a year. Some of these long-term unemployed have dropped out of the job market and are thus left out of the job-less statistics. Among those who have either retained their jobs, or found new jobs, many are working for lower wages. According to the NY Times[11],"One quarter of the jobs in

---

10 *True Progressivism,* The Economist, October 13, 2012

11 *The Rise of the Permanent Temp Economy,* NY Times, January 26, 2013

America pay below the poverty level for a family of four ($23,050). Not only are many jobs low-wage, they are also temporary and insecure." It is estimated that 50 million Americans are living in poverty, some unemployed, some employed at minimum wage (or below) jobs. Tens of millions of elderly are living primarily on Social Security pensions. These are among the "47% dependent, non-income-tax paying citizens" scorned by recent presidential candidate Mitt Romney.

The plan I have developed is a reflection of my views that political democracy cannot exist without social democracy and reasonable economic equality. Gross economic inequality leads to a society which is inevitably undemocratic. An example of this is the "Citizens United" decision by the Supreme Court and the resulting ability of the wealthy to spend a great deal of money to influence elections. This inequity can hardly be described as "one person, one vote", so fundamental to democracy. Another example of the impact of wealth is the lobbying of Congress to prevent necessary financial regulation and an equitable and fair tax code. However, this book is not an attack on economic success, only on the accumulation of wealth beyond any reasonable need, and how these riches are employed. There are examples, such as Bill and Melinda Gates, who have contributed generously to eradicating sickness on a world-wide basis. The Koch brothers, known as supporters of right-wing political causes, have also supported many worthwhile cultural and educational programs. The problem is that much of individual wealth is committed to supporting the continuing aggrandizement of the wealthy at the expense of the rest.

Before developing this fiscal plan I needed to establish the objectives which I believed such a plan should satisfy. While I will spend much of this book explaining my objectives, let me summarize them here.

1. Balance the budget. Eliminate the federal deficit.
2. Stimulate the economy, unlock a real economic recovery. Make American businesses more competitive.

3. Put people to work. Motivate bringing jobs home from overseas; increase domestic employment. Raise the minimum wage to a living wage.
4. Expand the social safety net for the sick, needy, infirm, and elderly. Fund these programs out of the General Fund, instead of a payroll tax. Reduce the total cost of health care (private plus public) while making it universally available.
5. Develop a tax code which is equitable, free of loop-holes and fair.
6. Reduce the wealth disparity. Provide the middle-class with increased disposable income.
7. Maintain a strong defense and anti-terror capability.
8. Provide foreign aid to growing democracies. Stay involved in world affairs.
9. Free-up the resources to deal with the problems of infrastructure repair/ replacement; global warming/climate change, renewable energy/ energy distribution; pollution/ habitat/ species destruction, and resource conservation.
10. Invest in the future - research & development, education, reduced global warming and preservation of the ecology.

One word I use freely in this book is "**equitable**". As I use it, equitable does not mean equal. It means fair, proportionate and balanced.

The United States economic crisis started with the recession in 2007/2008, but it has roots dating back many years. The causes were numerous. They include: a bursting housing bubble resulting in personal and financial industry liquidity problems; middle class salary stagnation; growing personal debt; an aging population; uncontrolled growth in the cost of medical care and college tuition; under-funded public pensions and retirement health insurance; wars in Afghanistan and Iraq, a cut in federal taxes and business competition from overseas. The results have been continuing government budget deficits and growing public debt; widespread, long-term unemployment and lack of new (decent) job opportunities; increasing disparity of wealth and income; and an increase in the number people living in poverty, receiving unemployment insurance and food stamps.

Initially, a great deal of money was injected into the economy by the federal government through low interest loans to the financial and automobile industries under the Troubled Asset Relief Program (TARP), and a $780 billion economic stimulus. While it is likely that these actions staved off a more serious depression, they did not end the economic crisis. More recently, the burden has largely fallen to the Fed to address the continuing economic problems through easing monetary policy. The short term interest rate has been reduced almost to zero and the long term rate to an historic low, essentially through the printing of money. So far, we have not experienced inflation from these actions, which, though fortunate, probably speaks to the underlying weakness of the economy. There are few monetary alternatives left for the Fed. It now remains for the President and Congress to address **fiscal policy**, and this involves more than **just** balancing the budget, or extending **another** fiscal stimulus. It takes a plan to address the larger economic questions.

The basic questions raised by the economic crisis are the following: Can Americans live as they have in the past, or must we make significant cuts in our standard of living to obtain fiscal stability? Has the American dream ended? How should we finance the future economic needs of America? What is equity in taxation and do we have the courage to make it happen? Can we educate our youth to meet the needs of the 21st Century, to compete in the world? Are our young people doomed to a life of minimal expectations? Has the economic leadership of the world passed to others? Have jobs moved overseas permanently? What would it take to regain our economic health? What can we do to stimulate the economy? And, while we are at it, can we provide universal health care to all and ensure a secure retirement to our elderly after a lifetime of work? **Can we abolish poverty in America?**

The plan presented in this book addresses all these questions. It responds, yes, we can address our problems: we can balance our budget, we can abolish poverty, we can regain our leadership in the world. **We can make ours a more perfect union.** Is it ambitious? Sure, but I believe there is enough wealth in this country to achieve a rebirth of the American dream if this wealth is more evenly distributed. It does not take a revolution to bring about the necessary changes. Many European countries already have pieces of this plan in place. Rather, as happened in the 1930s, it takes an evolution, a redefinition of democratic capitalism and political democracy. It will require sacrifice on the part some, particularly the wealthy, and commitment on the part of all. We can make America a kinder, gentler place to live.

Some have said that the budget should be balanced by making severe cuts in the social safety net: Medicare, Social Security, Medicaid, retired military health care, unemployment compensation, food stamps, and student grants. Others have called for another fiscal stimulus. I believe that balancing the budget through **cuts in the social safety net** or authorizing another **deficit-financed** financial stimulus unwise and unfair. Such actions, will, at best, complicate and delay the ultimate solution to the underlying problems. I believe the federal government must revise its fiscal policy consistent with our democratic ideals, and the sooner the better.

Long term, the United States, together with the rest of the world, faces problems of energy availability, limiting CO2 emission and halting climate change. The recent tropical storm Sandy which brought devastation and dislocation to the East Coast of the United States should be seen as a warning, "not of things that must be, but of things that might be"[12]. Dealing with these problems will take huge public investments in conservation, clean energy and energy distribution over the next few decades. In the present fiscal environment public capital is simply not available to address these issues. Continued delay will bring about energy shortages, serious climate change, and a reduction in the availability of food and clean water. Ultimately, these could lead to world chaos.

---

12 *A Christmas Carol,* Charles Dickens

During the 2012 presidential debates both candidates talked of improving the lot of the middle-class, growing the economy, adding new jobs and dealing with the deficit. Joel Klein summed up the frustration that Americans have had with both 2012 presidential candidates when he wrote, "[Presidential candidate] Romney's proposals for the next four years are ridiculous; the President's non-existent."[13] This book offers a plan for restructuring America's economy in FY2015 through changes in the federal fiscal policy (receipts and outlays). It incorporates elements from both liberal and conservative economic schools of thought. Many of these ideas have been offered separately by others at various times. Most noteworthy have been former Labor Secretary Robert Reich; Senator Bernie Sanders; and economists Joseph Stieglitz and Paul Krugman whose contributions to my thinking have been critical. This book takes a systemic approach, that is, it offers an integrated fiscal plan, and looks at the consequences and interaction of the various elements of the plan. It starts with the premise that **continued deficit financing is undesirable**...that we can, and should, balance the budget. It addresses: income/wealth disparity, stimulating the economy, providing jobs, eliminating poverty, broadening Medicare to cover all Americans, and financing both Medicare and Social Security by means of income taxes. The current financial crisis requires far more action than just bringing outlays and receipts into balance, although this is a good starting point. The nation's economy has not been challenged so thoroughly since the Great Depression in the 1930s. At stake is our system of **democratic** capitalism. The financial crisis is far from over. The price of housing is still deeply depressed with many owners under water on their mortgages and facing foreclosure. Unemployment is widespread...many abandoning their search for work or taking low paid jobs. Young people are getting out of college with heavy debts and few opportunities. Poverty is widespread, and Medicare and Social Security, which have kept tens of millions of seniors alive and out of poverty, are endangered. **We need to reaffirm**

13 Joel Klein, *A Campaign Without a Heart,* Time Magazine, October 29, 2012

our belief not just in the capitalist system but in democracy, in equality of opportunity, in our social commitments and in shared burden. The current economic crisis is an opportunity to redefine our nation in a way that has not happened since the Great Depression. This plan takes on that challenge.

And, a challenge it is. The subject of fiscal planning can either seem so complex that the public can feel overawed and abandon the field to the "experts", or, not really understanding all of the complexity, can fall into the trap of over-simplifying. Hopefully, this plan avoids both extremes. I have tried not to resort to slogans, or demonizing on one hand, or failing to see the forest because of the trees on the other. Yes, if the income tax code is to be rewritten it will ultimately need expert attention. But, before that, we need to define some broad principles. I fault our political leaders for failing to clarify the over-riding choices. The political ramifications of these choices and the influence of politics on our choices cannot be overlooked.

I start with the view that **a balanced budget need not imply an austerity budget.** I concur with President Obama that, "Deficit reduction alone is not an economic plan." Under this plan, increased federal outlays and significant reductions in business expenses are expected to serve as stimulants to the economy. Unlike the president's budget or that proposed by Mitt Romney or Representative Ryan, the federal outlays proposed herein are fully funded, primarily through an increase in upper-income taxes. Almost everyone, except those earning under $10,000 per year, will pay increased income taxes. Those earning under $125,000 per year will see the increase more than offset by the elimination of payroll taxes and a reduction in the cost of health care. The net tax increase is small for those earning between $125,000 and $250,000 per year. For most in this income range, the increase in taxes will be offset by the elimination of the cost of private health insurance, and reductions in the personal cost of family health care. Above this level the increases are larger, particularly for those whose incomes are derived from investments, deposited in tax shelters or who have received large deductions under the present tax code. This writer does not believe that raising taxes on upper income individuals will reduce the economic activity of this country. This conclusion is supported by the Congressional Budget Organization (CBO). "**CBO analyses indicate that letting the high-income [Bush] tax cuts expire would very likely *help* long-term economic growth if policymakers use the resulting revenues to help shrink deficits, as the President has proposed.**"[14] Letting the high-income (over $400-450,000 per year) tax cuts expire as recently agreed to by the President and Congress will reduce deficits by about $600 billion over the next ten years, ten-to-fifteen percent of the anticipated deficit during this period under present federal fiscal plan. The plan offered in this book calls for steeper increases in taxes for the wealthy. Some say this will depress the economy. I disagree...the effect of this action on the economy should be offset by the stimulus the plan provides to business, the increase in disposable income for the most people, and greater government outlays. Businesses and the banks are sitting on trillions of dollars in potential investment capital. The reduction/elimination of corporate taxes, payroll taxes and business funded health insurance will further increase available investment capital. Business needs the incentive of predictable growth in demand to expand, provide jobs and grow the economy. The growth in disposable income for the middle class through savings in the private cost of health care and, for the working class resulting from full employment and an increase in the minimum wage will help provide that incentive.

An article published in the Huffington Post Online on September 18, 2012, makes reference to speeches by President Obama and 2012 presidential candidate Mitt Romney. "In a leaked May campaign fund-raising video Romney called 47 percent of Americans 'dependent on government' since they don't pay federal income taxes." Obama, in a recording of a 1998 Loyola University appearance said, 'The trick is figuring out how we structure government systems that pool

14 *Claims About Economic Downside of Ending High End Tax Cuts Don't Hold Up*, Chye-Ching, Center for Budget and Policy Priorities, November 12, 2012

resources and hence facilitate some [wealth] redistribution – because I actually believe in redistribution, at least to a certain level to make sure everybody's got a shot." On September 18, 2012 the NY Times quoted Romney as saying in an interview on Fox News, "The president's view is one of a larger government; I disagree. I think a society based on a government-centered nation where government plays a larger and larger role, redistributes money, that's the wrong course for America." This plan includes provisions which address both these issues...the first, the phony issue, that "47% are dependent on government", and the latter, a real issue, "the redistribution of wealth".

There are many subjects which could have been considered in this book, including: the banking system (e.g. the Volker rule – prohibiting proprietary trading by banks), financial regulation (Strengthening and enforcing Dodd-Frank), accounting oversight, too-big to fail", monetary policy, equality of opportunity for women and minorities, free trade/ global economy, consumer protection (loans, mortgages and credit cards), the culture of greed, cronyism, manipulation of the commodity markets, and building a sustainable environment in a recovering economy. I have, however, limited the scope of this book to domestic **fiscal issues:** balancing the budget, taxes, income/wealth disparity, economic growth, education, housing, jobs and the social safety net. The problems we face are not unlike those faced by Bill Clinton during his presidency. He made the decisions to raise taxes and cut expenditures. Critics said this would bring on a recession. Instead the economy boomed and the deficit disappeared. This plan follows a similar pattern: increased taxes (primarily affecting the wealthy) while reducing some outlays. The proposed plan is, however, far more sweeping in scope than President Clinton's program. The choice America faces is not between a balanced budget and "entitlements", it is not between going right and left politically, it between doing right and wrong. **It is between fairness, equity, democracy, and privilege, inequity and oligarchy**. While this book offers a plan which calls for a wider safety net it also calls for steps to stimulate business, by reducing corporate taxes and eliminating corporate contributions to employee health insurance and Social Security. It calls for steps to end poverty and for steps to bring jobs back to America. It calls for increased taxes on the wealthy and for equity through the elimination of tax loop-holes.

This book is of necessity a work in progress. Change is happening so rapidly in the business world, in Washington and internationally that it is impossible to keep up. However, I believe the ideas embodied here are applicable independent of these changes, and that it is necessary to get the process started.

A. Deficit

The United States has run a significant annual deficit since 2007. It is projected a continued deficit into the foreseeable future. The Congressional Budget Office released the following figures for federal deficits:[15]

- 2007 - $161 billion
- 2008 - $459 billion
- 2009 - $1.4 trillion
- 2010 - $ 1.3 trillion
- 2011 - $1.3 trillion
- 2012 - $1.1 trillion
- 2013 - $845 billion (projected)
- 2017 - $535 billion (projected)
- 2021 - $845 billion (projected)

In FY2012 fully one-third of our outlays were based on borrowed money.

It amazes me to read what some economists say about our federal deficits. Dr. Paul Krugman, who I look to as a mentor, calls those who would eliminate the deficit, "deficit hawks". He believes that interest payments on the national debt are not excessive, and claims that "there was a lot of bad faith involved, as the deficit scolds tried to exploit an economic (not fiscal) crisis on behalf of a political agenda that had

15 *Budget Battles: Lower Deficits, Rising Tempers,* Time Magazine, February, 18, 2013

nothing to do with deficits."[16] Much as I respect Dr. Krugman, I disagree. (However, as you shall see, I do not disagree that we need an economic stimulus. I think we can balance the budget and provide a **funded** stimulus - read on.) The primary reason the continuing deficit/ national debt has proven manageable is that interest rates are close to zero. Let the rate rise to a more normal level and the interest on the debt will become a significant fraction of the government outlays limiting our freedom to address necessary areas such as clean energy, infrastructure repair and replacement, and education.

Dr. Alan Meltzer in his book *Why Capitalism?,* says, "The United States government is on a course in 2009, 2010 and 2011 to run the largest peacetime deficits in its history." Did you say peacetime, Dr. Meltzer? Tell that to the troops who fought in Iraq and Afghanistan. Tell that to the families of the thousands of Americans who died there and to the tens of thousands who have been wounded and maimed. As in every war in our history, we supported the wars in the Middle East with deficit financing.

On what does Dr. Meltzer blame the deficits? Largely, entitlements: Social Security, Medicare/Medicaid and Welfare. The facts are: 1) Social Security has been, and continues to be, self-supporting, funded through payroll taxes. It currently has a $2.5 trillion surplus. If we discontinued Social Security entirely there would be no change in the deficit. 2) Medicare and Medicaid[17] were designed from their inception to receive funding from the general fund. 3) The number of people on Welfare has been reduced during the past ten years from 14 million to 4 million. (All programs that receive funding from the general fund can be said to be "deficit financed" as long as there is a deficit, an absurd use of the term.) It is true that the costs of Medicare and Medicaid have increased significantly, but, **the cost of private insurance has increased even more rapidly**. The problem lies in the rising cost of

16 NY Times, January 24, 2013, *Deficit Hawks Down*

17 There is no doubt that the cost of Medicare and Medicaid are going up. This is due to the increase in medical cost in general and the ageing of the population. This will be discussed in a later section.

medical care in general and the aging of the population, not these programs. We need to address medical costs, but not by reducing Medicare or Medicaid coverage or benefits. (This book proposes expanding Medicare to cover everyone.) According to the NY Times[18], "A new report from a panel of experts convened by the Institute of Medicine estimated that roughly 30 percent of health care spending in 2009 — around $750 billion — was wasted on unnecessary or poorly delivered services and other needless costs. Lack of coordination at every point in the health care system is a big culprit." The problem of waste goes beyond "coordination" and inefficiency. It includes the overhead and profit of private health insurance which contributes little to health care. It includes exorbitant (and non-negotiable) cost for prescription drugs. It includes fraud and overcharging. Steven Brill[19] has estimated the following areas of "potential savings in the nation's health care system...without substituting the kind of government provider system typical in comparative countries: (substituting Medicare would permit even greater savings)

. $94 billion - Control of prescription prices, which make up 10% of U.S. health care costs. Studies show that drug prices in the U.S. are, on average, 50% higher than other developed nations,

. $84 billion - Recapture 75% of profits of hospitals, whose expenses are about a third of health care costs,

. $74 billion - Cut 5% from hospitals and physician costs by reducing the over-ordering of tests and other procedures,

. $50 billion - Spending on out patient clinics and labs owned by doctors could be cut by a third by regulating fees or taxing profits,

. $30 billion - Use transparency, price controls and whatever else it takes - to bring the overall gross profit margins of medical device makers down to 50%,

. $28 billion - Allow and fund comparative effectiveness evaluations in decisions to prescribe drugs, tests and medical devices.

---

18 *Waste in the Health Care System,* NY Times, Sept. 10, 2021

19 Steven Brill, Time Magazine, March 4, 2013, *Why Medical Bills Are Killing Us*

Dr. Meltzer is wrong. The deficit existed during the past decade primarily because President Bush chose to cut income taxes while taking the nation into two undeclared and unfinanced "wars" in Iraq and Afghanistan. The Defense Department budget went up 70% from 2001 to 2010. The deficit was further increased since 2008 by the financial crisis. As a result, the national debt has gone from 58% of GDP in 2000 to in excess of 100% of GDP today.

Whatever the reasons for the national debt, at over $16 trillion, it is in fact huge. This number is so big that most can't grasp its enormity. The debt is easier to understand when it is defined as $50,000 for each and every American...man, woman and child. It becomes meaningful when we are told we can't afford food stamps to help feed our hungry children, or when we are told we must cut Medicare and Social Security programs for the elderly.

I have listened with dismay to politicians, economists and pundits commenting on what should be done about America's on-going budget deficit ($1.1 trillion in 2012.) and the growing national debt. The suggestions for dealing with the deficit generally fall into three categories: 1) Ignore the deficit/national debt, it/they are not important. America can print all the money it needs…we can just "monetize" it. 2) Close some "loop-holes", move to a flat tax, reduce the size of government and cut entitlements. 3) Increase the marginal tax rate on the wealthy. These approaches, each largely intended to satisfy a particular political constituency, range from counter-productive to inadequate. I believe balancing the budget is important (witness what is happening in Europe). We have been borrowing to finance the federal government since the end of the Clinton presidency. Even Keynes would not have recommended indefinite deficit financing.

Some have offered plans to balance the budget. These have ranged from the simplistic 9-9-9 plan of Herman Cain (Herman who?), to the regressive and unrealistic plan of Congressman Paul Ryan, Republican vice-presidential candidate in 2012. His plan has been supported by Congressional Republicans and was largely supported by the Republican presidential candidate Mitt Romney. The Ryan plan cuts Social Security, replaces Medicare with vouchers, cuts Medicaid and veteran benefits, while decreasing taxes on the wealthy. He uses balancing the budget as an excuse for cutting social programs. This would not only deny necessary protection to the vulnerable in our society, but would exacerbate the economic problem. On top of this, he advocates cutting taxes. The revenue cost over the next decade of the tax cuts embodied in his plan is $4.6 trillion[20]. These cuts — which would be, by the way, over and above those involved in making the Bush tax cuts permanent — would disproportionately benefit the wealthy, with the average member of the top 1 percent receiving a tax break of $238,000 a year.[21] Despite these cuts, Ryan insists his plan is revenue neutral, but the nonpartisan Tax Policy Center has done the math, and the national debt would increase $4.3 trillion from these cuts over the next decade[22]. "The tax-cutting, entitlement-curbing budget that he drafted in 2011 would not balance the books until 2040"[23]. Ryan recently (March 2013) came out with a revised plan which taking advantage of the tax increase recently negotiated on the wealthy (which he opposed), and the provisions of the Affordable Care Act (which he says he would overturn) would balance the budget by 2023.)

Republican Senator Tom Coburn says "Medicare is unsustainable[24], Social Security is unsustainable[25], discretionary spending is unsustainable and the Defense Department is

---

20 Estimated by the non-partisan Tax Policy Center

21 Common dreams, 4/9/2012

22 Paul Krugman, New York times, August 19, 2012

23 *A Fiscal Hawk Grounded,* The Economist, October 20, 2012.

24 It is not that Medicare is unsustainable. Rather it is that the growth of medical costs in general is unsustainable, whether privately funded or publically funded. According to the Economist, June 16, 2012, America spends 18% of it GDP on health care, of which about one-third is waste.

25 Social Security, funded by the payroll tax, has been self-sustained for 75 years. It could continue sustainable into the indefinite future by an increase in the maximum limit on taxable income. However, this paper, proposes that future funding be transferred to income taxes, an equitable, progressive and sustainable means of funding retirement for America's elderly.

unsustainable." I disagree. I believe **with a fair and equitable tax code, and by making judicious savings in outlays, we can afford these programs**. Grover Norquist offered the "No tax increase pledge" to further stultify the process. (Every Republican candidate for President in 2012 supported this idea.)

The most serious effort to balance the budget was made by the Bowles-Simpson U.S. Deficit Committee. Their plan failed to win approval, able to muster only 38 affirmative votes in Congress. The plan proposed was not sufficiently innovative, was indefinite, and its many compromises jeopardized its ability to win the support of either the conservatives on the right or the liberals on the left. Economist Paul Krugman commented, "The fact is that Simpson-Bowles [also known as Bowles-Simpson] is a really bad plan, one that would undermine some key pieces of our safety net. Many progressives oppose its proposed savings from Social Security and Medicare. Many conservatives resist proposed tax increases and military cuts. Officials in the White House and in Congress grouse that few Bowles-Simpson fans are aware of particulars, like new gasoline taxes and higher capital gains taxes on inheritances. And critics say the chairmen have oversold the idea, which Republicans have embraced, that Washington can raise revenues by curbing popular tax breaks instead of raising tax rates."[26]

In February, 2013 Erskine Bowles, a Democrat, and Alan Simpson, a Republican came out with a revised plan. The Huffington Post quotes Jeff Sprouse as saying this new plan, "represents a massive shift away from their own previous target and towards more spending cuts." It would seem to be time for these two to give it up.

B. Debt/Debt Ceiling/Fiscal Cliff

1) Debt

"The federal debt has two components. One is "debt held by the public", which consists primarily of U.S. Treasury Bonds that anyone

26 NY Times, November 27, 2012, *Now touring, the Debt Duo, Simpson-Bowles*

can buy. Most of this debt is held by the Federal Reserve, state and local governments and the American public, but a substantial amount is owned by foreign governments.

The second component is intergovernmental debt where one part of the government borrows from another. The best examples of this are Social Security [about $2.5 trillion] and Medicare [about $300 billion] trust funds."[27] All told. About $4.5 trillion out of a total debt of about $16 trillion of the federal debt is due to intergovernmental debt. (This book proposes to fund Social Security and Medicare - among others - out of the general fund. If this were adopted $3 trillion of debt would immediately disappear. (How's that for fiscal magic?)

If you have difficulty understanding this accounting I recommend reading *The People's Guide to the Federal Budget,* A National Priorities Project. What does it mean for the Fed to purchase government bonds? Where does the money come from? Does purchasing these bonds reduce the federal debt? And, what does intergovernmental debt really mean? Congress has set a debt ceiling and refuses to raise this limit without numerous spending concessions. What does this mean after Congress autorized the expenditure of these funds?

2) Debt Ceiling

Perhaps the most immediate impact of the fiscal cliff was to have been the debt ceiling. Initially expected to be exceeded by January 1, 2013, due to fiscal manipulation by the Treasury and the Fed, the debt ceiling would probably not officially have been breached until the end of February, 2013. Dealing with this crisis has been a challenge for the President and Congress. Amendment XIV, Sec. 4 to the Constitution says, "The validity of the public debt of the United States, authorized by law...shall not be questioned." Under this Amendment, I (and many others) believe the President has the responsibility and the authority to ignore the debt ceiling (which

27 http://www.facingup.org

would appear to be unconstitutional), to declare a national emergency and continue paying our bills. The question has been, did he have the will? (Appearing on CBS' Face the Nation, on Sunday, January 6, 2013, Minority Leader Nancy Pelosi offered her endorsement of the 14th Amendment option, which she held that therefore Congress doesn't have the power to use the debt ceiling as a hostage-taking device because the validity of the debt "shall not be questioned". The 14th amendment option was gaining popularity among Democrats on the Hill. Senate Majority Leader Harry Reid (D-NV) urged the president to deploy it when the two were contemplating the contours of the just-completed fiscal cliff debate.)[28] The President, however, has indicated he does not plan to use this option.

Faced with the President's position that he would not negotiate another debt ceiling, "the House passed a delay in the limiting the statutory borrowing until May, without the dollar-for-dollar spending cuts the Republican's once insisted would have to be part of any debt ceiling limit bill."[29]

3) The Fiscal Cliff

"A bear came over the mountain,
A bear came over the mountain,
A bear came over the mountain,
And, what do you think he saw?
He saw another mountain,
He saw another mountain,
He saw another mountain,
And, what do you think he did?
He climbed right over that mountain..."
Ref: Children's ditty

28 Sam Stein, Huffington Post, January 6, 2013, *14thAammedment Option*

29 NY Times, January 23, 2013, *House Vote Sidesteps an Ultimatum on Debt*

In 2011, a Congressional "Super-committee", tasked to reduce government outlays, failed the necessary majority for a consensus, leaving a legacy of more-or-less arbitrary and dangerous automatic spending cuts to be implemented in 2013. (The could lead to layoffs of tens of thousands of teachers, closings of national parks, reductions in food inspections, and cutbacks at the FBI and the Border Patrol. The budget cuts required would reduce defense spending significantly, and reduce domestic spending even more.)[30] These automatic cuts, known as "sequestration", were put in place so that Congress would be "forced to act". (See below.) Despite its flaws, I believe the plan for sequestration, together with the end to the Bush tax cuts, was a better plan than Bowles-Simpson. At least everyone knows that going over the fiscal cliff would not resolve America's fiscal problems, while Bowles-Simpson claimed to offer a solution without even really recognizing many of the problems.

Because of the inability of the Democrats and the Republicans in Congress to agree on a fiscal program for 2013, by the end of 2012 the economy was rapidly approaching what has been dubbed a "fiscal cliff" (a term invented by Fed Chairman Bernanke). Expected to occur by January 1, 2013, the actions were postponed to the end of February, 2013 by an agreement between the President and Congress. According to the Economist[31], "The fiscal cliff exists because several temporary measures [were] set to expire at the same time. George W. Bush's tax cuts, which were extended for two years under Barack Obama, [were] due to run out. So [were] Mr. Obama's temporary jobs measures, such as a payroll tax holiday [affecting 100 million Americans. Indeed, this was allowed to run out in the recent agreement.]" The agreement is referred to in a recent article from the NY Times as the Biden-McConnell Plan - See below.) Thanks to the failure of a Congressional Super-committee to agree on a debt-reduction deal last year, automatic cuts in federal spending [were to have been] due to start on January 15. 2013."

30 NY Times, July31, 2012

31 The Economist, *Business and America's Fiscal Cliff,* October 6, 2012,

a. Sequestration

In an article published on The National Law Review entitled, *Fiscal Cliff, Taxmageddon, Sequestration - What does it all mean?*, Jeremy R. Scott defines "Sequestration" as "a rarely used procedure in budget related legislation that allows for automatic cuts in federal spending." Under the current sequestration, "federal budgets would be reduced annually by roughly $110 billion to meet the deficit reduction goals, [$1.2 trillion over 10 years] with cuts split more-or-less evenly between Defense and non-Defense spending. The entitlement programs and military pay and veteran services are largely exempted. Some believe the effects on the economy would be severe. Others argue that it involves a small cut in the GNP and would therefore have a small effect. Sequestration was to go into effect on January 15, 2013 if in the event that a bipartisan group of Senators and Representatives known as the 'Super Committee' failed to agree on $1.2 trillion of spending cuts." The intention was to force a deal to reduce the deficit.

The Super Committee was unable to come to agreement and sequestration was scheduled to start. On January 1, 2013 agreement was reached to extend the effective start date by two months. (See the McConnell-Biden Plan below)

The Washington Post reported on February 5, 2013, "President Obama called on Congress to pass a small package of spending cuts and tax changes to delay the start next month [March, 2013] of deep reductions in domestic and defense spending that could deliver a fresh blow to the fragile economic recovery. With time running out, Obama said, Congress should adopt measures to postpone the automatic spending reductions...for a few months."

On February 6, 2013 the Huffington Post reported that, "President Barack Obama is asking Congress for a short-term deficit reduction package of spending cuts and tax revenue that will delay the effective date of steeper automatic cuts now scheduled to kick in March 1, [2013]." I believe that this delay should be until the start of the next fiscal year in October, so that the President and Congress may have the time to work out a new budget for next year. Another short-term delay makes little sense. Even more important, this would give the President time to propose a long-term fiscal plan starting in FY 2015 which could be fought out in the 2014 Congressional election.

On March 1, 2013 the Sequestration went into effect. The initial reduction for FY2013 is $85 billion for the seven months ending in September, 2013. Most entitlements, such as Social Security and Healthy Care are excluded. The biggest cuts are in defense with a rough equivalence in the rest of the discretionary programs.

The state governments have been hit severely by the sequestration. For example: Massachusetts will lose an estimated 80 million dollars in FY 2013 in the areas of Human Services, Education and Labor alone. This translates into thousands of jobs. Other states will suffer proportionately[32].

b. Compromise

There was a continuing call for compromise in December, 2012 as we approached the cliff. A short-term compromise, reached at the last minute on January 1, 2013, called the McConnell-Biden Plan, is summarized below. It largely just delayed the problems for two months. (The plan proposed in this book offers a far more comprehensive approach. It calls for raising taxes on the wealthy; stimulating the economy and increasing private employment through tax reduction and cost savings for business; and expanding the social safety net. The various elements support each other in an overall systemic and fair approach.)

The McConnell-Biden Plan[33]

A last-minute deal, forged between the Senate Minority Leader, Mitch McConnell, and Vice-President Joseph R. Biden Jr., passed

32 Senate Appropriation Subcommittee on Labor, Health and Human Services

33 NY Times, January 2, 2013

in the Senate early Tuesday morning and in the House late Tuesday night, January 1, 2013. The legislation prevents hundreds of billions of dollars in tax increases set to kick in for the majority of Americans and temporarily suspends scheduled automatic spending cuts.

Almost unnoticed was the fact that a whole series of benefits for private firms was also slipped into the bill. For example, The NY Times reported,[34] "Just two weeks after pleading guilty in a major federal fraud case, Amgen the world's largest biotechnology firm, scored a largely unnoticed coup on Capital hill: Lawmakers inserted a paragraph into the 'fiscal cliff' bill that did not mention the company by name but strongly favored one of its drugs. The language buried in Section 632 of the law delays a set of Medicare price restraints on a class of drugs which includes Senispar. It is projected to cost Medicare up to $500 million over that period."

What Was Included:

Income tax rates: Maintains current rates on income below $400,000 for singles and $450,000 for couples. Permanently increase tax rates on income above that to 39.6 percent from 35 percent.

Dividend and capital gains rates: Permanently increases tax rates to 20 percent from 15 percent for single people with incomes over $400,000 and couples over $450,000.

Exemptions and Deductions: Reinstates provisions that phase out personal exemptions and deductions for incomes over $250,000 for singles and $300,000 for couples.

Alternative Minimum Tax: Permanently indexes the alternative minimum tax for inflation, preventing millions of taxpayers from being affected.

---

34 NY Times, January 19, 2013, *Fiscal Footnote: Big Senate Gift to Drug Maker,* by Eric Lipton and Kevin Sack

Estate tax: Permanently increases tax rates to 40 percent from 35 percent on the value of estates above $5 million.

Tax Credits: Extends tax cuts in the 2009 stimulus law for five years, including a child tax credit, an expanded earned income tax credit and a refundable credit for college tuition. Some business tax credits were extended.

Payroll Tax Increase: Allows payroll taxes to rise on Tuesday to 6.2 percent from 4.2 percent on workers first $113,700 of income.

Unemployment Insurance: Extends expanded unemployment insurance for one year.

Medicare provider payments: Prevents a 27 percent reduction in payments to Medicare providers for one year.

Automatic spending cuts: Delays for two months the $110 billion in automatic spending cuts set to go into effect in 2013, paid for with unspecified cuts elsewhere.

Farm bill extension: Extends for nine months portions of the current farm bill, including provisions that would prevent milk prices from increasing and continued direct payments to farmers. Eliminates conservation programs and financing for fruit and vegetable growers and organic farmers and does not include disaster assistance.

What was left out:

Debt ceiling: The country officially hit its debt limit on Monday, December 31, 2012, and the Treasury is undertaking "extraordinary measures" to put off default. If Congress doesn't raise the ceiling by late February or early March the Treasury will not be able to pay all of its bills. (The NY Times reported on January 18, 2013," House Republicans said on January 18, 2013, that they would agree to lift the federal government's statutory borrowing limit for three months, with the requirement that both chambers of Congress pass a budget in that time to clear the way for negotiations on long-term deficit reduction." The decision represents a victory - at least for now" the Times said, "for Mr. Obama, who has said for months that he will not negotiate budget cuts under the threat of debt default.") Earlier proposals by President Obama and speaker Boehner included hundreds of billions more in deficit reduction, with Mr. Obama favoring increased taxes on the wealthy and Mr. Boehner favoring spending cuts.

In any case, long-term compromise does not seem possible. The Republicans are still on the path to reducing the size of government at any cost. "The Reagan/Thatcher vision of limited but competent government regressed to the notion that any government is bad except when it comes to defense spending or regulating social conduct. But, Reagan always recognized a role for government in protecting society's most vulnerable."[35] Responsible fiscal planning has given way to a battle over ideologies. Unfortunately, these issues did not get a thorough airing during the recent election debates. Two years ago, President Obama missed an opportunity to move toward a balanced budget when he agreed to extend the Bush tax cuts.

Time Magazine[36] points out that, the budget proposal offered in 2012 by President Obama and the Republican-controlled House Budget Committee each call for the government in 2021 to spend a trillion dollars more than it spends today. The proposal offered here calls for the government to spend one-half trillion more in FY2015, providing a significant fiscal stimulus. The differences lie not just in

35 *Why Republicans Should Help Obama Succeed*, Sheila Bair, Fortune Magazine, December 24, 2012

36 *Bubble on the Potomac,* by Andrew Ferguson, Time Magazine, May 28, 2012

the time frame, but, in what the money is to be spent for, and equally important, where it is to come from.

The fiscal cliff (more accurately a fiscal slope since for the most part, it would have taken effect gradually, except for the debt ceiling, which as I described can be accommodated) was in fact less a crisis, than it is an opportunity. No one wished to see the draconian cuts scheduled for the end of 2012 take affect but most of them would have been reversible in 2013. The partial reversal of the Bush tax cuts of McConnell-Biden provided an increase in revenue and the opportunity to address equity in income taxes not as an increase for the wealthy, but as a reduction for the middle class. (This gave the "no tax increase" Republicans semantic cover.) The appearance of a cliff gave the president negotiating power. The Republicans realized that the President is in an even stronger position in 2013 now that the new Congress has taken office. He should have insisted on a fiscal plan which constitutes a long-term, balanced fix to the economy. President Obama is by nature a compromiser, but this is not the time for compromise. The unemployment rate in November, 2012 fell to its lowest level in four years, 7.7%. The NY Times points out, that "the job growth suggests that most employers aren't yet delaying hiring because of the "fiscal cliff."[37] So, business did not seem to be too worried about this crisis. If the Republican Congress refused to go along the president he should let the axe fall, allow the negotiated debt-reduction plans go into affect and take his case to the people. When the Republicans again make the debt ceiling an issue, he should declare a national emergency and initiate emergency measures through executive orders. In any case, many of the changes will actually take place over a period of time, not suddenly, as the term "cliff" implies and are reversible. (Despite the term "permanent" used by many in Congress, taxes are always subject to change.) The president has the opportunity to make history...to join in the line of great presidents extending from Washington through Jackson, Lincoln, Theodore and Franklin Roosevelt, Harry Truman and

37 The New York Times, December 7, 2012, by AP, *November Jobs Report*

Lyndon Johnson. But, to do so he has to stand firm against the latest call for compromise. In the immortal words of Yogi Berra, "It ain't over 'till its over."

c. Another Mountain

On February 28, 2013 the U.S. Senate voted down opposing plans to avert the across-the-board cuts known as sequestration (See above). This would appear to be the last opportunity to avert a cut in the budget of $85 billion this year. According to the Huffington Post, Senate Majority Leader Harry Reid warned of the following consequences, "hundreds of thousands of civilian employees of the Defense Department will be furloughed...families and businesses across the country are also bracing for the pain of deep cuts to programs that keep our food safe, our water clean and our borders secure." The failure to reach an agreement was hardly a surprise. Time Magazine reported in the February 18, 2013 issue, "President Obama and House Speaker John Boehner returned to their old postures: threatening economic harm to the nation if they don't get their way on deficit reduction - this time by way of $1 trillion [over 10 years] in poorly planned automatic cuts set to take effect on March 1, 2013."

President Obama blamed Republicans for failure of Congress to reach an agreement to stave of the sequestration. Speaker Boehner said the Democrats would have to agree to post-sequestration spending cuts. Once again business and investors do not seem terribly concerned. In fact, on March 5, 2013 the Dow Jones Industrial Average reached a new high. It is beginning to look more and more like the sequestration is more important to politicians than to most people.

C. Employment

The discussion on reducing unemployment is particularly disappointing. Stagnating working and middle class incomes and widespread unemployment has had a major impact on the overall economy and on individual lives. The presidential election was probably decided based on this issue more than any other. (If you cannot support your family other concerns tend to vanish.) Unemployment has been variously estimated to be between 7.7 and 18 percent of the available work force, depending on who is being counted. Do we count only those actively seeking employment, or include: those who have given up and dropped out of the work force, part time employees who would like to work full-time, and those who have accepted lower paid jobs? The number of employed people fell by almost 120,000 from July to August 2012, continuing a long-term trend. According to the Bureau of Labor Statistics the number of employed people in the US fell from a peak of 146 million in November 2007 to 142 million in August 2012. This is partially due to the retirement of many baby boomers. But, it is also due to the increasing rate of discouraged job seekers, the loss of manufacturing jobs and the increase in the number of disabled workers partially due to the aging of the population.

Fifty million people, including children, live in, or close to, poverty. (According to Census Bureau figures, one out of every five American children lives in poverty. For blacks and Hispanics, it's one out of every three.) The Supplemental Assistance Nutrition Program, better known as SNAP, and even better known as Food Stamps, currently has around 46 million participants, a record high. That's more than one in eight Americans. The U.S. poverty rate grew from 11.3% to 15.0%, a 33% jump, in just 11 years. The impact was felt primarily by minorities and women. The median wealth for single black and Hispanic women is shockingly low, at just over $100, compared to $41,500 for single white women[38]. Many of the heads of poverty households **are employed at low-paying jobs**. The current federal minimum wage is $7.25. The President has recommended raising it to $9.00 per hour. If the minimum wage had kept up with inflation since it was established in 1968, at $1.60, it would today be set at $10.55 per hour. I believe it should be set at this level. While

38 Common Dreams, October 11, 2012

some states and municipalities have higher minimum wages than the federal rate, many do not.

The suggestions on how to improve the job market fall primarily into two categories: 1) Injection of money into the economy by the federal government through another fiscal stimulus, continued low interest rates and/or further Quantitative Easing (QE) by the Fed (The Economist labeled this, "printing money to buy bonds[39]). On June 20, 2012 the Fed pledged to buy $267 billion in long term treasury bonds over the next 6 months as part of a campaign to reduce borrowing costs. It is not at all clear that additional QE would have much effect. QE primarily is intended to reduce the long-term interest rate. However, the long term interest rate, currently at 1.7%, is already near a record low. The policy of flooding the economy with capital and keeping the interest rate low has been beneficial to the stock market, but has done little to reduce the deficit or to bringing down the unemployment rate.[40](Investors need only look to 2012 as an example. The domestic economy has grown at an annual pace only slightly above 2 percent, subpar by historical standards. Overseas, the picture is worse: Japan is teetering on the brink of yet another recession, large parts of Europe's economy are contracting and China's pace of growth has slowed uncomfortably. Yet against this bleak backdrop, United States stocks have returned 15 percent, on average, while those in Europe have gained 18 percent and Asian stocks are up more than 12 percent.)[41]

In the United States, those in the top 10% of the income distribution own more than 80% of all public equity outstanding.[42] On September 12, 2012, according to the NY Times, "The Fed said it would add $23 billion of mortgage bonds to its portfolio by the end of September, and set a pace of $40 billion in purchases a month. It

---

39 *Investors, Beware,* Economist, October 6-12, 2012

40 NY Times, September 29, 2012

41 NY Times, *The Economy and Stocks, A Big Disconnect,*Paul J. Lim, December 15, 2012

42 Economist Magazine, *Trickle-down Central Banking,* October 10, 2012

promised to announce a new target at the end of September, 2012, and every subsequent month, until the labor market outlook improves 'substantially', as long as inflation remains in check. It did not further explain either standard."[43] (As promised, planned purchases were increased in September to $85 billion per month for the last three months of 2012.[44]) These actions mean a continuing deficit, a growing national debt, and potential long term inflation. Perhaps because of Congressional gridlock, the president and his financial advisors have consistently relied on the Fed to "fix" the economy. It has limited affect. 2) Establishing a more favorable financial climate for business investment, primarily through reduced taxes on the wealthy to encourage the private sector to add jobs through private entrepreneurship. There is no evidence that this trickle-down approach to employment will work. Few jobs were added as a result of the Bush tax cuts. A far more direct and far-reaching approach is required.

D. Poverty

"I continue to believe that the unwillingness of our national leadership to engage the nation in a straightforward discussion of American poverty is corrosive. We proclaim our commitment to opportunity for all, but, shoving one child in five under the rug in our national discourse makes a mockery of that declaration."

Peter Edelman in his book *So Rich, So Poor,*

No fiscal plan can be considered complete without addressing the distribution of wealth in the United States. Over 400 individuals currently have a net-worth of over a billion dollars. More will be said about this end of the wealth scale below in the discussion of a Net-worth Tax. However, before going into such detail it important to recognize that almost 50 million Americans are locked into abject poverty. "Nine million people fell into poverty between 2007 and

43 The New York Times, September 29, 2011

44 ibid

2010, an astonishing 20.5 million people lived in extreme poverty in 2010 (earning less than $9,000 per year, ½ the poverty line), up by nearly 8 million in ten years." [45]While some efforts have been made to help these individuals...Food Stamps, Medicaid, Earned Income Tax Credit...the situation has only grown worse. And the cost of these programs is not negligible, amounting to over $100 billion a year. The Economist notes that, "America's poor face systemic challenges beyond the aid of any single administration or program...The low-wage jobs that many used to climb out of poverty in the 20th Century are largely gone. Deteriorating family structure among the poor threatens to trap poor children at the bottom of the income ladder for life."[46]

Mitt Romney may have destroyed his candidacy with his criticism of the bottom 47% of the income distribution as dependent and not paying taxes. He failed to note that many of these people were working poor who paid payroll taxes but did not earn enough to owe any income tax. Others were retired people who lived on Social Security and depended on Medicare for their health care. His fiscal plan would have penalized these people by reducing their benefits. Republican pressure continues after the election to reduce entitlement and food stamp cost. This book calls a very different approach. It offers a plan which would provide employment to all who are capable of and wish to work; and increases the minimum wage to raise working people out of poverty. It provides Medicare to all through government sponsored, single-payer health insurance and pays for Social Security out of the general fund. Both of these programs would be financed by raising income taxes, primarily on the wealthy.

Poverty blight's our society. It leads to broken families, educational drop-out, and crime. It jeopardizes our democracy. The United States has the second highest poverty rate among OECD countries, following Mexico. The elimination, or at least significant reduction, of poverty is a primary objective of the plan presented in this book.

---

45 *So Rich, So Poor,* by Peter Edelman

46 The Economist, November 10, 2012, *In Need of Help*

Part 2. Taxes

"Compared with other developed countries, the United States has very low taxes, little income redistribution, and an extraordinarily complex tax code. If it wanted to, the government could raise taxes without crippling growth or productivity. Tax reform is ultimately a political choice, not an economic one—a statement about what sort of society Americans want."

Andrea L. Campbell, Foreign Affairs Magazine, September – October, 2012.

A. Current Problems

Taxes are the way we generate the major portion of the revenue needed to pay for government operation and services. Politicians, under pressure from special interest groups, have established a tax code which is unfair, complex[47] and desperately in need of revision. It is full of loop-holes, places a disproportionate burden on the middle class, and taxes "earned" income more severely than other income. Under the existing budget, revenue is inadequate to cover outlays resulting in deficits[48] and a growing national debt. The way we allocate taxes is a direct expression of government policy. Who should bear the burden of financing government operations and in what proportion? What activities do we wish to motivate or discourage? What will stimulate or retard economic activity and what kind of activity do we wish to favor?

47 The most recently published Tax code, from February, 2010, had 3,837,105 words according to the Congressional Budget Office.

48 President Obama's budget for 2012 includes a deficit exceeding 8% of GDP.

The intent of this plan is not to deny people the fruits of their labor, creativity, or frugality. Economic incentives are extremely powerful and wealth is a reasonable reward for these attributes. Exorbitant wealth however, beyond that needed for comfort (even luxuries) and financial security for individuals and their families is unnecessary, and dangerous in a democracy. Great family wealth has been preserved for generations through effectively low income and estate taxes.[49] Raising taxes on the wealthy can help to balance the budget, make the tax burden more equitable, reduce the disparity in wealth between the super-rich and average Americans, and reduce the influence of money on our political system. "No serious proposal to take the money out of politics, or even reduce its tightening grip on the body politic, emerged from the [Party conventions in Tampa or Charlotte], so the sounds of celebration and merriment are merely prelude to a funeral cortege for America as a shared experience. A radical minority of the super-rich has gained ascendency over politics, buying the policies, laws, tax breaks, subsidies, and rules that consolidate a permanent state of vast inequality by which they can further help themselves to America's wealth and resources."[50]

I do not blame Mitt Romney, or the other multimillionaires, for paying as small a fraction of their incomes in federal taxes as the law allows, while others who earn far less pay twice as much. (I do, however, resent his disparagement of 47% of Americans for paying no income tax, having a victim mentality and being dependent on the government. According to the Economist Magazine[51], "Over half

49 The combined Estate Tax obligation for all estates filing estate tax forms in 2010 was $13 billion. The final filing threshold was $5 million. There are 31 billionaires in the USA worth over $10 billion each. You would think that if just a few of these died the total estate taxes would exceed $13 billion. Not to mention the 400 people worth more than $1billion or the 250,000 worth over $5million. What happens to all the inherited wealth? Among to the Forbes 400 billionaires, approximately 40% inherited their wealth.

50 *Money in Politics: Where is the Outrage?* Bill Moyers and Bernie Weisberger, Commondreams.org

51 The Economist, September 22, 2010

those he condemned have jobs and pay payroll taxes but earn too little to be subject to income tax as well. Another 20% are retired. Only 8% of households pay no federal tax at all, usually because their members are students, disabled or unemployed.") I suspect most taxpayers take advantage of all the loop-holes available to them. I do not blame the wealthy for using their money to influence elections and legislation. I blame our elected and appointed officials for a tax code which make it possible for the top 1% to pay so little tax and for laws which permit the use their wealth to unduly influence our political processes. (No, Mister Justices, money is not speech, corporations are not people and super-PACs are not independent of the candidates they support.)

Every major candidate for the Republican nomination for President has been wealthy, and/or has had one, or more, super-PACs or billionaires backing his candidacy. The Democratic and Republican candidates were similarly supported in the fall election. It is estimated that $2.6 billion was spent in media advertising[52] during the 2012 Presidential election campaign. Congressional candidates are reported to have spent $3 million, on average, on their campaigns.

Reducing taxes on the working class will provide them with increased purchasing power which will be a stimulus to the economy and help lead to increased employment.

B. Simplification

In an article in Fortune Magazine, April 9, 2012, entitled, *Your IRS FAQ*, Stanley Bing writes, "No taxation without obfuscation. It's the American way." While this is a tongue-in-check view of the tax code, there is a great deal of truth in it. "The tax code", he writes, "is more than 3 million words long [3,837,105 as of February, 2010] and would fill 7,500 pages if printed on letter-sized paper."

There has been a great deal of discussion about "simplifying" the tax code. Much of the discussion is nonsense, an attempt to justify lower taxes for the wealthy by calling for a flat tax. A flat tax is not

52 Anthony DiClemente, Barkley Capital

any simpler than a progressive tax. In one case you multiply your taxable income by the flat tax rate. In the other, you look up your taxes in a table. What we need is not a system of equal taxes, but, one of **equitable taxes.** One of the other words which have been much used by politicians when they discuss taxes is the word "fairness". Ultimately, fairness is in the eye of the beholder. We are all influenced by our own positions in life. Let me be clear, my view is not that everyone should pay the same tax, or even proportional taxes. I believe that **those who earn higher incomes should pay a greater portion of that income than those who earn less.** Why? Because I think it is fair, I think it is democratic, and I think it makes for a better society.

The complexity of the tax code is primarily related to the calculation of taxable income. (Just to further complicate things, we have the Alternative Minimum Tax and the Earned Income Tax Credit. Under this proposed plan these would be eliminated. The much discussed "Buffet Tax" would be unnecessary.) We frequently hear the argument that we should close "loop-holes". What's a loop-hole? For many the answer is: **A loop-hole is a deduction, exemption or credit that someone else gets**. (The government calls these "tax expenditures", a misleading term. The OMB estimates that tax expenditures in fiscal 2012 resulted in revenue loss of $1.1 trillion.[53]) Very few of us consider our own deductions loop-holes. I consider virtually all "tax expenditures" to be loop-holes, and accordingly, believe **we should eliminate all special exemptions, credits and itemized deductions**, with the only exceptions being a $10,000 exemption for everyone (replacing all itemized deductions), limited inheritance and net worth exemptions (assuring the maintenance of a basic level of wealth), and, necessary and actual business expenses. Is that simple enough? (There are hundreds of deductions, allowable expenses, carry-overs, exemptions and gimmicks in the present tax code. Only 1/3 of the taxpayers,

53 The Economist Magazine, 4/28/2012

primarily the wealthiest, make use of most of the existing deductions, the remainder choosing not to itemize.)

Many of these expenditures are designed to motivate questionable "socially desirable behavior" or to favor a particular group, e.g. farmers and homeowners. I believe that the use of the tax code, by way of deductions, credits and exemptions to motivate behavior such as deductions for charitable contributions, having children and owning homes, should be ended. The favoring of one particular group over other taxpayers is totally unjustified and has no reason for existing except for politics. These deductions are arbitrary and discriminatory. They benefit some individuals at cost to others.[54] (After all, someone has to pay the bills.)

There are arguments which can be made for every exemption. Perhaps, the most controversial deduction is the charitable one. According to the Economist Magazine, June 9, 2012, "Over half of American's charitable contributions go to religious organizations, typically attended by the donor, and thus could be interpreted more as a fee rather than an act of charity." (There is also the question as to the constitutionality of this deduction.) The charitable deduction is one many people will defend. After all, aren't these organizations doing good work? Please don't misunderstand me. I am not suggesting you stop contributing to your favorite charity. I am only suggesting the tax deduction be eliminated. Let's take a look at the typical deduction. Suppose Mr. and Mrs. Goodwill make a contribution of $100 dollars to their favorite charity. (The term charity is used broadly. It may be charity for the giver, but the receiver need not be involved in doing charitable work. It could be an educational institution, a cultural one or any of a large number of tax-deductible causes. However, I will keep using the term charity so there is no misunderstanding.) If the Goodwills are in the 25% tax bracket this contribution will, under the current tax code,

54 According to The Economist Magazine, 4/26/2012, The bottom 40% collectively enjoy just 11% of all tax expenditures, primarily those for children, earned income and education expenditures. 75% of the preferential rate on capital gains and bonds go to the top 1%.

cost them $75 dollars. Assuming they itemize, $25 comes back to via a tax deduction. The charity, however, receives $100. Where does the extra $25 come from? The answer is from you, me and the other tax payers, because we have to make up in additional taxes what they failed to pay. So we, the tax payers, have in effect, jointly made a contribution to Mr. and Mrs. Goodwill's favorite charity, **whether we support the objectives of that charity or not.** Why should the Goodwills determine where our charitable contributions go? They should not.

It is quite likely that eliminating the tax deduction for charitable institutions will result in a reduction to the contributions received by many organizations. They may, in turn, have to reduce their services. Colleges and universities, for example, may reduce their scholarship programs. To some degree this could be offset by increased government grants. In some cases, the organization may not be eligible for a grant, and may have to survive on the lesser contribution or end up going out of business. Well, that's capitalism...if you don't offer a service people are willing to pay for you go out of business. Of course, these grants will cost additional money. In any case, I think it preferable that our elected officials determine where our money goes rather than the Goodwills.

Many of the other so-called deductions are equally questionable. The deduction for interest paid on a home mortgage is clearly discriminatory. Renters get no such deduction. The recent housing bubble should make us rethink the desirability of encouraging home ownership for all. The deduction for having children (already not available to high income taxpayers) is counterproductive. In an environmentally stressed and overpopulated world we should be encouraging people to limit their family size rather than expand it.

While we think about these more "personal" deductions, there is also the non-profit designation of any number of groups organized to influence the political process. Much of the money spent in support of candidates on a national and state level is collected and dispersed by organizations which have managed to get themselves classified as "not for profit" public interest groups. These groups do no have to report their source of contributions. One of these, ALEC, has been extremely effective in changing state law to favor particular corporate interests. (It is, however, classified as a non-profit organization rather than a lobbying organization.) The elimination of the designation "nonprofit" for such groups would have very salutary impact on American politics.

If states and municipalities followed suit, they could proceed to eliminate the tax exemptions of so-called nonprofits, easing their budget problems. Again, these exemptions cost all of us additional taxes, whether we support their objective or not. For example, it appears to me that all property held by other than the government should be subject to the same taxation. Some of the prime property in New York City is owned by religious organizations and universities. These are private entities, albeit their educational and social objectives may be desirable. Attendance is limited only to those who qualify. They do not serve the "general welfare" and should be self-supporting. (Additionally, much of the property private colleges sit on was given to them as land-grants.) I emphasize that this does not mean they are not worthy of individual contributions. Much the same can be said about art and cultural groups. While a segment of the population derives benefits from these they are still largely limited to their particular constituencies. Needless to say, private entities such as sports teams should not be subsidized by public funds. (Localities may choose to give tax benefits to business on the basis that the jobs provided or local benefits such as income or tourism justify the outlay. That is up to them, but the federal government should not be involved in these decisions or expenditures.)

"As negotiations to avert the [delayed] fiscal cliff intensify [the first round has ended], corporate lobbying groups are pushing key tax perks that benefit the wealthy. A coalition of financial institutions, fossil fuel companies, telecommunications firms and even the cigarette company Altria are teaming up to block a tax increase on dividends, a policy that overwhelmingly aids the rich. When a company turns a profit, it can either hold onto its money to invest in new projects or pass on the money to its shareholders as a dividend. Provided this stock has been held for at least a few months, and is issued by a U.S. company, these dividends currently qualify for the special 15 percent tax rate on capital gains, rather than the higher tax rate on ordinary income, which is currently 39.6 percent for the wealthiest Americans. Over 50 percent of all capital gains over the past two decades have accrued to the wealthiest 0.1 percent of taxpayers, according to The Washington Post, while the richest 5 percent of Americans receive 80 percent of all capital gains."[55] Under this plan the special rate for dividends, as well as that for capital gains would be abolished. Off-shore tax havens would be eliminated. (This latter provision alone might nullify up to $100 billion a year of tax avoidance.)

I would like to see deductions totally eliminated. Others have suggested capping them. One value suggested is $50,000, which the Tax Policy Center estimates would yield $748 billion over ten years. Where did $50,000 come from? Certainly it is not designed to protect the middle class. An alternative would be to cap deductions at some lower value. "During the presidential campaign, Republican nominee Mitt Romney suggested limiting itemized deductions to a dollar cap, such as $25,000. The nonpartisan Tax Policy Center estimates that capping deductions at $25,000 would raise $1.3 trillion, but, 29 percent of it would come from those earning under $200,000, whose taxes both parties say they don't want to increase."[56] I suspect the bulk of the deductions over $25,000 for the middle class are associated with retirement plans and mortgage interest

The following chart identifies the largest tax expenditures in fiscal year 2012:

55 The Huntington Post, December 11, 2012

56 Las Vegas Sun, December 9, 2012

Anticipated Tax Expenditures, 2012

Rank	Tax Expenditure	Billion $
1	Employer contributions for medical insurance premiums and medical care	171
2	Capital gains and dividends	97
3	401K, IRA and self-employed pension plans	93
4	Mortgage interest	87
5	Accelerated depreciation	76
6	Employer pension plans	44
7	Deferral of tax on foreign profit	42
8	Charitable contribution	33
9	State and local Taxes	33
10	Municipal bond Interest	29

Source: Office of Management and Budget, as reported in The Economist Magazine, 4/28/2012.

C. Income Tax

1) Taxable Income

What should be classified as taxable income? I propose all income in cash or otherwise (at the value thereof), with no distinction between "earned" and "unearned" receipts, and no special treatment for the source of the income. Taxable income would include: salaries, fees, bonuses, perks, stock and stock option awards, profit distributions, deferred earnings distributions, interest, dividends (with no exceptions), realized capital gains (The definition of "long-term capital gain", with reduced tax rates, as property held more than just one year is totally illogical), pensions (company pension contributions would be considered deferred income), insurance and trust fund receipts, gifts, and inheritances[57]. Payments made under the proposed single-payer health insurance would not be taxed as income to the beneficiary since they go directly to the health care provider not the beneficiary. Of course, for the health care provider they are income. (The first $1.28 million inherited by a spouse and each child would be exempt. Due to this exemption, taxing inheritance as income will effect the wealthiest only. The tax impact of this plan on spouses would be further mitigated through joint property ownership.)

I know that the argument will be made that if we eliminate the capital gains tax advantage people will stop investing. I don't believe this. There are simply no alternatives. Bond and saving interest rates are so low as to be almost non-existent. Few will keep their money under their mattress. A reduction of the corporate tax (see below) will encourage the growth of American businesses and enhance the profitability of investing in equities.

Income taxes would be due from every US resident, and, from American citizens living and working overseas or domestically.

2) Income Tax Rates

Under this plan income would be taxed progressively[58]. For each individual, $10,000 of income, or the first $10,000 for higher income earners, would be exempt. (Thus, your child would not have to pay taxes on his/her allowance or gifts received up to a total of $10,000 per year. Social Security benefits, or other pensions for those with no other income up to $10,000, would also be untaxed. Currently, the tax code allows up to $5,000 in pensions to go untaxed for single senior citizens.) Income $10,000 - 20,000 would be taxed at the marginal rate (that portion of income between $10,000 and 20,000) of 15%, partially replacing payroll taxes for low earners.

57 Only 15,000 estate tax returns were filed in 2010, according to the Congressional Budget Office. After accounting for marital and charitable bequests, expenses and debts, less than half of those filling in 2010 owed estate tax.

58 "The median income for a household headed by a person age 55 to 65 in 2010 was $56,575." AARP Bulletin, March 2012.

(See below.) Income of $20,000 - 40,000 would be marginally taxed 20%; $40,000 - 80,000, 25%; and so on. The marginal tax rate would increase by 5% each time income doubled, up to a maximum marginal rate of 50% for income over $1,280,000 a year. Each person's income would be individually taxed, whether married or single. (The maximum marginal tax rate for single filers under President Ronald Reagan was 50%. Since then, income for the wealthiest 1% has gone up by 300%, while the maximum marginal rate went down to 35% for taxable income over $379,150.[59] It has recently been increased to 39.6% for those earning over $450,000. Due to the loop-holes in the present tax code the 400 wealthiest Americans, all billionaires, actually only paid an average rate of 18.1% in 2010.)

Will raising the marginal tax rate on higher income individuals be counter-productive, causing them to stop working, or reduce their efforts, and thereby reduce revenue? Not likely. Under this plan, even the highest paid individuals will get to keep over 50% of their incomes. (The amount of income retained would be reduced by foreign, state and municipal taxes.) While income is important, it is hardly the only reward. People in high paying jobs also receive personal satisfaction and enjoy the power and prestige that goes with the job. I expect for every high paid executive who decides to stop work there will be ten qualified people in line for the job.

3) Examples

I have selected the 2012 presidential and vice-presidential candidates to illustrate how the recommended income tax code would affect high income earner tax rates. These examples are based on their released their income tax data.[60] They could, under this plan be subject to the net-worth tax (see below) but since their net-worth has not been released no estimate is provided here for this tax. The

59 Economic Policy Institute

60 New York Times, August 17, 2012

estimates for the political figures shown is not based on a detailed analysis.

The first of these is the super-wealthy Mitt Romney. He claims to have paid at least 13% of his income in taxes for the past 10 years. (What percent have you paid?) He belatedly released his 2011 income tax information. In 2011, Romney and his wife paid income tax at the rate of 14.1% on a total income of $13.7 million. (In 2010 his income tax rate was 13.9% on an income of $21.6 million.) Under this plan, Romney's tax rate would more than triple.

Romney's running mate, Congressman Paul Ryan, and his wife, earned a more modest income of $323,416 in 2011. He paid income tax at a rate of 15.9%. Under this plan his tax rate would more than double.

President Obama and his wife paid income taxes of $162,074, at a rate of 22% in 2011 on a declared income of $728,674 (down from $1,728,696 the previous year, as his book sales slowed). His rate would approximately double under this plan.

Vice-president Biden and his wife earned a taxable income of $379,035 in 2011. They paid $87,000 in taxable income in 2011, a rate of 23%. Under this plan their tax rate would also approximately double.

Under the proposed income tax plan each of these families would see their tax rates increase significantly. (At least the President and Vice-president have said their rates ought to increase.) Romney would also pay a 5% wealth tax on his net worth of an estimated $200 million. The good news for each of these families is that they, and their children, would all be immediately eligible for single-payer health insurance under this plan, and each could receive full Social Security benefits at the age of 67. (See below.)

In order to illustrate how ordinary citizens might be affected in fiscal 2014 three fictional tax payers have been considered as follows:

a. Middle-class family of four - earnings from employment, one parent $100k per year, second parent $50k per year. In addition, the family earns $500 from investments. Under the proposed tax code this family will save $3,497 this year.

	Current Tax Code	Proposed Tax Code
Income		
Salary	$150,000	$150,000
Investment	500	500
Personal deduction	7,400	0
Standard Deduction	27,100	0
Taxable Income	$122,700	$150,500
Outlays		
Income Tax	22,110	37,176
Payroll Taxes	9,275	0
Medical cost	11,485	2,297
Total	$42,870	$39,473

b. Retired single person - income - $15k Social Security, pension $20k, income from investment/savings $3,500 per year. Under the proposed tax code this individual would save $6,247 this year.

Current Tax Code	Proposed Tax Code	
Income		
Salary	0	0
Pension	$20,000	$20,000
Social Security	15,000	15,000
Interest/dividends	3,500	3,500
Standard Deduction	7,250	0
Personal Deduction	3,700	0
Taxable Income	$27,550	$38,500
Outlays		
Income Tax	2,897	2,900
Medical Expenses	7,000	750
Total Expenses	$9,897	$3,650

c. High income couple - One person - $2.5M from employment, other person 0. In addition the couple earns $500k from investments. The proposed tax code would cost this couple $376,000 more this year. (This does not include any net worth tax they may owe.

	Current Tax Code	Proposed Tax Code
Income		
Salary	$2,500,000	$2,500,000
Investments	500,000	500,000
Itemized Deductions (Est.)*	1,000,000	0
Taxable Income	2,000,000	3,000,000

* Includes state and municipal taxes, real estate taxes, interest on mortgage, sales tax, tax free bond income, IRA contribution, foreign taxes, etc.

	Current Tax Code	Proposed Tax Code
Outlays		
Medical Expenses (Est.)	20,000	4,000
Taxes		
Payroll	196,000	0
Income (Est. @ 28%)**	560,000	1,248,000
Total	$876,000	$1,252,000

** Average over all income

4) Tax Rate Comparisons

How would the tax rates compare in this proposal to 2012 Income tax brackets? The following table shows the comparison for Single Filers, Married filing Separately, Married filing jointly, and Head of household: Comparison is complicated by the multiplicity of 2012 Tax brackets. The comparison is most easily made to Single Filer since that is the only category in this proposal. (In this proposal, not only are all sources of income treated equally, no advantage or disadvantage is associated with marital status or household arrangement. It should also be noted that for most people earning less than 113,700, their tax liability will be reduced 6.2%, by elimination of the Social Security payroll tax and 2.35% (Increased by 0.9% in 2013 under the affordable care Act) by the elimination of Medicare payroll tax. Self-employed individuals will save even more. Only those earning over $250,000 will see significant increases in their net payments. It is expected that most individuals with incomes less than $125,000 per year will see their net payments reduced, while those earning between 125,000 and 250,000 will be unchanged (Federal income tax rate minus payroll tax rate minus health care costs). The amount of the change in their net cost will depend on whether they are self-employed or salaried, their current deductions, exemptions and exclusions, the source of their income (salary or investment) and who pays for their current health insurance.

Comparison 2012 Tax Rate/Brackets[61] vs. Proposed Rate/Brackets

	Current (2012) Marginal Bracket*				Proposed fiscal 2015
Tax Rate %	Single Filers	Married Filing Separate	Married Filing Joint	Head of Household	Bracket Individual
0	0-5	0-5	0-10	0-5	0-10
10	5-8.7	5-8.7	10-17.4	0-12.4	N/A
15	8.7-35.6	8.7-35.4	17.4-70.7	12.4-47.5	10-20
20	N/A	N/A	N/A	N/A	20-40
25	35.3-85.6	35.4-71.3	70.7-142.7	47.3-122.3	40-80
28	85.7-178.7	71.4-108.7	142.7-217.5	122.3-198.1	N/A
30	N/A	N/A	N/A	N/A	80-160
33	178.6-388.3	108.7-194.2	217.5-388.4	198-388.4	N/A
35	Over 388	Over 194.2	Over 388.4	Over 388.4	150-320
40	N/A	N/A	N/A	N/A	320-640
45	N/A	N/A	N/A	N/A	640-1,280
50	N/A	N/A	N/A	N/A	Over 1,280

*All brackets are in thousands of dollars.

61 IRS Tax Table

The fact that "head of household" would be no longer recognized as a separate tax category does not mean that it would not exist. Thus, money spent by an individual on his or her partner or children for reasonable and actual living expenses would not constitute income for those parties. This would include: food, shelter, clothing and educational expenses. Money received from outside parties would, however, constitute income. For example, a scholarship awarded to a student would have to carry with it the basic tax on that income as if it were the only income that individual received. This would prevent large gifts to pass as tax-free scholarships.

D. Corporate Tax

According to Time Magazine, "Corporate taxes are the most abused of all taxes. While the current corporate tax rate is nominally 35%, companies actually paid an average of only 12.1% in 2011. The rate reflects firms' deft use of loop-holes. Multinational corporations have more tax avoidance tools than ever. In 2010, corporations accounted for 9% of the nation's tax receipts. Our proposed solution is to eliminate corporate taxes and instead boost the tax rate on dividends and capital gains."[62] Some of the largest corporations already pay no corporate taxes.

I would reduce the corporate taxes in two steps. First, I would cut the base tax rate to 20% and eliminate all deductions except reasonable and actual cost of doing business. (Foreign, state and municipal taxes would be considered a cost of doing business. Now, U.S. corporations get a credit against their U.S. taxes for foreign taxes paid.)

Corporations that are American for all practical purposes would be prevented from avoiding U.S. taxes by claiming to be a foreign company, and corporations would pay taxes on off shore profits as they are earned[63]. The reduction to 20% will help to compensate for the elimination of loop-holes, equalize the tax burden on all corporations (reduce some/raise some) and could actually realize more revenue than the present 35% rate does (12.1%).

---

62 Time Magazine, Feb. 20, 2012, *Economy Briefing*

63 These provisions have been proposed by the Sanders/Schakowsky Corporate Tax Fairness Act

I would reduce a corporation's tax rate an additional 5 points for every 1% increase in their domestic full-time employment sustained for the taxable year. This should serve as an incentive to bring cash home and to expand domestic employment. Approximately 50 million American workers are employed in small business having on average 25 workers. A small business corporation, employing 25 or fewer people, could reduce its corporate tax rate to zero by adding one additional employee. If one half of these companies added one domestic worker per year employment would increase by one million workers per year. Companies increasing their domestic employment in excess of 4%, and maintaining this employment, would be eligible to carry over the tax reduction to the following year. This would be an enormous stimulant to small business.

Larger corporations could participate in this program also. They too might be able to expand their domestic workforce by one million employees. (They start with a base almost twice as large as small businesses.) Imagine if the domestic employment could increase by two million employees in one year! One of the claims is that there are not enough skilled workers in the United States to fill the jobs already available. These are jobs that in many cases do not require a college education, but do require training. This plan would allow companies to offer apprentice programs at little cost to them (The cost would largely be covered by the saving in corporate taxes.) to develop the skilled labor they need.

In other chapters of this book I will discuss increasing the purchasing power of the American public, which will be needed to justify this increase in jobs.

1) Fees/Special Taxes

I would assess realistic fees on businesses for the use of public assets such as water, public land, mineral rights or the radio spectrum, and for the clean-up of any pollution they may have caused.[64] These fees would help to assign the true cost of a product or service.

64 AOL on line, December 30, 2021.

I would institute a carbon tax to motivate the use of low carbon energy sources and low carbon footprint products. It is estimated that a carbon tax could raise up to $80 billion in FY2015, and as much as $310 billion by 2050.[65] Senator Bernie Sanders writes, "A proposed tax on carbon emission would reduce the use of fossil fuels that contribute to climate change, encourage U.S. companies to move to cleaner forms of energy use, increase efficiency of existing fossil fuels, and help develop new technologies. Individuals and households would receive rebates to reduce or eliminate the impact of this tax on their energy bills. The revenue raised would be used to help invest in clean energy technologies and solve our budget problems."

On February 14, 2013, Common Dreams.org reported[66], "Senators Bernie Sanders and Barbara Boxer introduced two separate bills, the Climate Protection Act and the Sustainable Energy Act, calling for a fee and dividend program, which would impose a fee on processed carbon (i.e. at the oil refinery, coal processing plant, etc.) by levying a per tonnage and returning three-fifths of the revenue generated to the public in the form of a rebate." This could be a start of a plan to assess fees on the use of "the commons' which could offset the reduction of corporate taxes.

I would also assess a financial transaction tax (FTT) to help curb excessive speculation.[67] (This is a tax which the financial services industry can easily afford to pay, having made an estimated 40% of all business profits in 2011, while providing about 8% of the GDP. I believe this

---

65 IBID

66 *'Carbon Fee & Dividend' Bill Introduced to Battle 'Planetary Emergency' of Climate Change,* Jon Queally, staff writer, Common Dreams.org, February 14, 2013.

67 The Bank for International Settlements reported in 2008 that annual trading in derivatives had surpassed $1.14 quadrillion (a thousand trillion dollars!). The Chicago Mercantile Exchange handles about 3 billion annual contracts worth well over a quadrillion dollars. One-tenth of one percent tax of a quadrillion dollars could pay off the deficit on its own. More conservative estimates by the Chicago Center for Economic Policy Research suggest FTT revenues of half-trillion dollars annually. I have assumed revenues only half of this lesser amount in this plan.

tax will be absorbed by the American financial industry rather than passed along to their clients and risk driving these transactions overseas.) According to The Economist, "Eleven Euro states are expected to institute an FTT, starting in 2014. France is already partly there. In August, [2012], it enacted a 0.2% tax on the purchase of French firms with a market capitalization of over one billion Euros among other things."[68] It is estimated that a 0.25% FTT could raise as much as $50 billion/year.

Together, these fees could raise as much as $400 billion annually, more than offsetting the loss of revenue from reduced corporate taxes. Corporate profits would eventually be taxed as income when distributed to stock or bond holders as dividends, interest or buy-backs and to employees as compensation. (The question of taxing corporate dividends and buy-backs is admittedly complex. Corporations today are international in scope. They may be incorporated overseas and/or foreign-owned and still do business in the U.S. Similarly, Americans may own shares in foreign corporations. The tax code would have to be structured to be sure that internationally derived and distributed income is fairly taxed and to prevent avoidance.)

I believe in free-market capitalism. But, to retain a free-market, business must be properly regulated. Teddy Roosevelt (a Republican) taught that monopolies were a direct danger to a free market in that a fundamental element of capitalism is competition. While capitalism offers the opportunity for great reward it also must carry the risk of failure. Allen Meltzer in his book, *Why Capitalism?,* observes that "capitalism without failure is like religion without sin. It doesn't work well." The recent emergence of the concept of a "too big to fail" enterprise is a direct challenge to this concept. Meltzer also notes that capitalism is not good at ensuring virtue.

We have seen the manipulation of markets, dishonest reporting and forecasting, and numerous failures in fiduciary and public responsibilities. As part of the plan of reducing corporate taxes, and improving the business climate, we should also fix the financial regulatory system. It should be dedicated to making corporate

---

68 The Economist, December 15, 2011, *Skimming the Froth*

organizations transparent, honest, and (as well as their executives) accountable. (Barofsky, a former watchdog for the U.S. government's financial system bailout in 2008, told Reuters that no individual or institution had been held meaningfully accountable for their role in the financial crisis. "Without such accountability, the unending parade of megabank scandals will inevitably continue," said Barofsky, who has been an outspoken critic of the government's response to the financial crisis.[69]) It should simplify and unify the regulatory process. The Economist magazine[70] describes the multiplicity of entities currently investigating and prosecuting financial firms in America. This results in "a deluge of paperwork in involving hundreds of subpoenas a week on average." This is costly for both the financial and regulatory institutions, and makes for confusion in responsibility. This cannot be beneficial to the public, the government or the financial institutions.

We should correct the deficiencies in corporate governance, emphasizing increased stockholder control. We should then stop trying to limit the level of compensation of business executives or financial employees (unless they are requesting or receiving financial assistance from the government), leaving the decision up to the stockholders. In any case, under the revised income taxes proposed in this plan, the public will receive a larger share of this compensation through equitable taxes.

The reduction of corporate taxes would help to compensate non-profit corporations which derive income from commercial properties for reductions in contributions which might result from the elimination of the charitable tax deduction (See below). It would also reduce the motivation for companies to shift profits overseas to countries with lower tax rates and to fail to bring profits home where they could be invested domestically or distributed to stockholders.

---

69 Commondreams.org, August 10, 201

70 Economist Magazine, *Law and Disorder,* October 13, 2012

2) Nonprofit Organizations

"A nonprofit organization or not-for-profit organization, often called an NPO or simply a nonprofit, is an organization that uses surplus revenues to achieve its goals rather than distributing them as profit or dividends. States in the United States defer to the IRS designation conferred under United States Internal Revenue Code Section 501©, when the IRS deems an organization eligible. Section 501© of the United States Internal Revenue Code (26 U.S.C. § 501©) provides that 28 types of nonprofit organizations are exempt from some federal income taxes."[71]

Nonprofit charitable organizations are exempt under Section 501(c)(3) of the Internal Revenue Code. Other tax-exempt organizations covered in this section include those exempt under Sections 501(c)(4) through 501(c)(9). Descriptions of these organizations are below:[72]

501(c)(3)	Religious, educational, charitable, scientific, or literary organizations; testing for public safety organizations. Also, organizations preventing cruelty to children or animals, or fostering national or international amateur sports competition
501(c)(4)	Civic leagues, social welfare organizations, and local associations of employees
501(c)(5)	Labor, agriculture, and horticultural organizations
501(c)(6)	Business leagues, chambers of commerce, and real estate boards
501(c)(7)	Social and recreational clubs
501(c)(8)	Fraternal beneficiary societies and associations
501(c)(9)	Voluntary employee beneficiary associations

71 Wikipedia

72 IRS Website

Nonprofit 501(c) 4, Social Welfare Organizations - Also often referred to as Super PACs, although not actually Political Action Committees at all, are instead IRS recognized 501(c)4 Tax Exempt Social Welfare Organizations formed for the purpose of improving the Social Welfare of society. There are also some limited cases where 501(c)5 (Union) or 501(c)6 (Business) Organizations are also formed for similar purposes. These organizations may use their funds for political advertising that supports their purpose as long as that political activity is not the primary purpose of the exempt organization. These types of organizations have no limits on the dollar amount of contributions. 501(c) 4 Social Welfare Organizations also differ dramatically from Political Action Committees, Super PACs and 527 Hybrid Super PACs in their ability to accept contributions that are not disclosed publicly. Examples of 501(c)4 Super PACs are Patriot Majority USA and Crossroads GPS.[73]

According to Public Citizen, "During last year's election, Karl Rove's Crossroads GPS spent more than $70 million to influence your vote. The Koch brothers' Americans for Prosperity: more than $39 million. The U.S. Chamber of Commerce: more than $36 million. Unlike super PACs, these and similar dark money groups are not required to disclose the identities of the corporations and super-rich donors that paid for the misleading ads they ran."

With the elimination of the federal tax deduction for contributions to nonprofit organizations and the reduction (potentially to zero) of federal corporate taxes there would be little-to-no difference between a for-profit and a nonprofit corporation. Individual states may continue to offer property tax deductions to such organizations and state income tax deductions (I would recommend against them) to those who contribute to such organizations. The residual 20% federal corporate tax proposed above would offer some advantage to being a nonprofit, tax-exempt organization. However, I believe the tax exempt status should be eliminated for all but government organizations. This would include religious organizations and non-public educational

73 Tax.freecharty.com

organizations. I see no reason why an organization such as Harvard University, which has an endowment of $35 billion, should not pay taxes on the income from invested endowments. Student aid and/or approved research would be allowable costs which would subtract from income. (See Section IV, Education, below.)

I don't know about you, but one of my long-term gripes is going to pick up my mail and finding that ¾ of the letters I receive on any given day are from non-profits, some of which I have never heard of and some that I have contributed to last month. The waste of paper is enormous. Once again last year the Post Office indicated it was operating at a loss. The solution they have arrived at appears to be two-fold: 1) the price of a first-class stamp is going up, and 2) mail deliveries will cease on Saturday. Non-profits can afford this deluge of mail because they get a very low mailing rate. The elimination of the designation "non-profit" would put an end to this, and with it remove much of the burden of mail delivery. It might even make the Post Office solvent.

But mail is only half my complaint...the other is the telephone. I am solicited daily, frequently by organizations I already support. Being on the "do not call" list does not help, since charitable organizations and political organizations are apparently exempt. I think that during the last election campaign I averaged at least one call a day asking me to vote for someone, even though I had told previous callers I already supported their candidate. So, another benefit to eliminating the non-profit designation would be peace and quiet.

E. Payroll Tax

"FICA is a regressive flat tax, beginning on the first dollar earned up to the first $113,700 in paycheck incomes for FY 2013, and there are no deductions. While nominally split between the employer and employee, the effects of the higher costs of employment are "passed through" to employees, who end up bearing the brunt of the employer side of the tax, in the form of lower wages, employer incentives, etc."

Ref: http://democraticchub.com/posts/88330/fiscal-cliff-deal is pro-cyclical-and-dangerous.

Carlos Bam-Bam, Dallas TX Posts, 1125, dated 01/04/13.

Payroll, or FICA, taxes currently pay for Medicare (partially) and Social Security (totally) for the elderly. Taxes are assessed on earned income only. The current rates are: 1) Social Security – 6.2% each, for employee and employer, up to a maximum of $113,700 annually. 2) Medicare - 1.45% each, for employer and employee, with no upper limit. I would eliminate Payroll Taxes[74] and fund Medicare and Social Security out of the General Fund. Eliminating Corporate and Payroll Taxes would provide additional capital to business for expansion, R&D, and modernization; and make American businesses more competitive with foreign companies by reducing the cost of doing business. Please note: I would eliminate FICA (Payroll) taxes - Social Security and Medicare – not the programs. When first established, Social Security was funded separately, as President Franklin Roosevelt said, "to give the contributors a legal, moral, and political right to collect their pensions." Unfortunately, he was wrong when he added, "With these taxes in there, no damn politician can ever scrap my Social Security program." Clearly, Social Security, and Medicare (authorized under President Johnson) have been under attack politically. Already the age for retirement under Social Security has been moved out to 67. It should go no further. The recent payroll tax holiday puts the program at increased risk. Why are these programs funded by a separate tax, a tax which is regressive and unfair? It now seems these programs would be more secure, and the funding less regressive, when funded out of the General Fund. (In the long run, these programs can only be protected by a ground-swell of public support.) Eliminating Payroll Taxes[75] would constitute a significant loss in revenue. This loss of revenue would be made up through increased income taxes described above. Under this proposed plan,

74 Medicare and Social Security Taxes

75 In 2008 Payroll Taxes constituted 36% of the Federal revenue.

for low income individuals income taxes would be more than offset by the elimination of Payroll Taxes and a reduction in their cost of health care. (See below.) For middle class tax payers, the increase in Income Taxes would be offset by the elimination of Payroll taxes and much of their present cost for health care. The increase in income taxes for the wealthy would go toward offsetting the loss of Payroll taxes, paying for government funded health care for all and toward providing Social Security payments out of the general fund.

F. Entitlements

1) Health Insurance

"[The Affordable Care Act] wasn't the health reform many were looking for. Rather than simply providing health insurance to everyone by extending Medicare to cover the whole population, we've constructed a Rube Goldberg device of regulations and subsides that will cost more than single-payer and have more cracks for people to fall through."

***The Big Deal,* Paul Krugman, NY Times, January 20, 2013**

"We sit together in a room in a modern emergency department in a rich country, a land where highly trained specialists confidently wield the newest technologies and expensive pharmaceuticals. But these treasures are not accessible to all, for ours is also a land where private health insurance is bought and sold as a commodity. Ours is a system known to shake down sick people for money they don't have. Ours is the only wealthy democracy that fails to guarantee health coverage to all of its citizens." Dr. David Dvorak.[76] A 2009 Harvard study published in the American Journal of Public Health found more than 44,800 excess deaths annually in the United States due to Americans' lacking health insurance. Fifty million Americans have no health insurance.

76 Quoted on Commondreams.org, 8/6/12

The Affordable Health Care Act will make major improvements in theses statistics. January 1, 2014 is the date at which the law's main parts take effect. Implementation will be complex and controversial. Exactly what the reality of the reform will amount to is still unclear. Its primary goal is to expand health insurance coverage; everyone must buy insurance or pay a penalty. Those with preconditions cannot be refused coverage. Medicaid will be extended to of those earning up to 138% of the federal poverty level. The bill provides subsidies to those with incomes between 100 and 400 percent of the poverty level ($15,415 for one adult). States, however, may choose whether to expand Medicaid as defined by this law. Initially, the federal government will cover the increased cost of Medicaid...eventually; it will cover 90% of this cost.

A better solution would be to provide medical insurance coverage to all under a revised Medicare program, often referred to as single-payer. (Vermont has the first state single-payer law, but it still lacks provisions recommended herein. Hawaii and California are taking steps in the direction of single-payer or a state-based public option.[77]) Clearly, such a program would require a significant expenditure of federal funds. These funds must be provided, deficit funding would be unacceptable.

In 2010 the U.S. spent $2.6 trillion on health care. This is a considerably larger fraction of GDP (18%) than other developed nations spend. The federal government share of this bill was about $820 billion, about 5.7% of the GDP, less than one-third of the total 18%. Under current law the breakdown of cost for health care in the U.S. will be as follows in 2020: Federal cost - 31%, State and local cost - 18%, Households - 26%, Business - 18%, Other - 7%.[78] Fareed Zakaria, in his article in Time Magazine, March 28, 2012, entitled, *World View,* compares cost and outcomes for the US and other developed countries. He notes that the average cost of an angiogram in the U.S. is $798, Canada $35; average life expectancy in the U.S.

77 Public citizen Health Letter, May 2012

78 Economist, *Looking to Uncle Sam*, July 2011.

is 78, Italy 82; the percentage of adult population with diabetes in the U.S. 10%, U.K. 4%. While there are numerous factors which contribute to these differences, they are sufficiently dramatic as to warrant investigation. **It is not just the cost of Medicare that needs to be controlled...it is the cost of medical care in general, if the United States is to achieve economic stability.**

a. Medicare

[79]Medicare has four parts:

- **Part A,** Hospital Insurance - helps pay for inpatient care in a hospital or skilled nursing facility (following a hospital stay) some home health care and hospital care.
- **Part B,** Medical Insurance - helps pay for doctors' services and many other medical services and supplies that are not covered by hospital insurance.
- **Part C,** Medicare Advantage - plans are available in many areas. People with Part A and B can choose to receive all their health care services through one of these provider organizations under Part C.
- **Part D,** Prescription Drug Coverage - helps pay for medications doctors prescribe for treatment.

The AARP Bulletin of November, 2012 reported, "In 2000, 40 million Americans, mostly elderly, received benefits under the Medicare program. By 2030, this number is expected to rise to 80 million. Experts project that Medicare will not be able to fully cover hospital costs in 12 years." What to do?

Under the proposed plan Parts A, B, and D in extended form would be covered under a single-payer program. Part C would be unnecessary.

79 U.S. Social Security Administration Website

b. Medicaid

[80]Medicaid is the United States health program for certain people and families with low incomes and resources. It is a means-tested program that is jointly funded by the state and federal governments, and is managed by the states. People served by Medicaid are U.S. citizens or legal permanent residents, including low-income adults, their children, and people with certain disabilities. Poverty alone does not necessarily qualify someone for Medicaid. Medicaid is the largest source of funding for medical and health-related services for people with limited income in the United States.

Unlike Medicare, which is solely a federal program, Medicaid is a joint federal-state program. Each state operates its own Medicaid system, but this system must conform to federal guidelines in order for the state to receive matching funds and grants. The matching rate provided to states is determined using a federal matching formula (called Federal Medical Assistance Percentages), which generates payment rates that vary from state to state, depending on each state's respective per capita income. The wealthiest states only receive a federal match of 50% while poorer states receive a larger match.

Medicaid funding has become a major budgetary issue for many states over the last few years, with states, on average, spending 16.8% of state general funds on the program. If the federal match expenditure is also counted, the program, on average, takes up 22% of each state's budget. Some 43 million Americans were enrolled in 2004 (19.7 million of them children) at a total cost of $295 billion. In 2008, Medicaid provided health coverage and services to approximately 49 million low-income children, pregnant women, elderly people, and disabled people. Federal Medicaid outlays were estimated to be $204 billion in 2008.

Medicaid does not pay benefits to individuals directly; Medicaid sends benefit payments to health care providers. In some states Medicaid beneficiaries are required to pay a small fee (co-payment)

---

80 Wikipedia, *Medicaid*

for medical services. Medicaid is limited by federal law to the coverage of "medically-necessary services".

Under the plan proposed, Medicaid would be folded into a single-payer health insurance program sponsored by the federal government and paid for out of the General Fund.

c. Tricare

Tricare, formerly known as the Civilian Health and Medical Program of the Uniformed Services (CHAMPUS), is a health care program of the Department of Defense Health System. Tricare provides civilian health benefits for military personnel, military retirees, and their dependents.[81]

Under this plan Tricare would be eliminated for all but service connected injuries. The remainder would be folded into a universal single- payer plan. Few people other those who have been connected with the military are aware of this program. It is funded under the Defense Department authorization, and today comprised approximately 10% ($50 billion annually) of the Defense Department budget.

d. Federal Employees Health Benefits Program (FEHB)

The FEHB is a system of "managed competition" through which employee health benefits are provided to civilian government employees and annuitants of the U.S. government. Workers pay one-third of the cost of insurance; the government pays the other two-thirds. It includes members of Congress.[82] This plan cost approximately $40 billion annually. Under the plan proposed, this program would be folded into Single-payer Medicare.

81 Wikipedia

82 *Federal? employees Health Benefits Program,* Wikipedia

e. Single-payer Health Insurance

In the 2012 Presidential election Americans faced a choice of two different visions of health care in the future. President Obama's is largely embodied in the Affordable Care Act. Governor Romney said he would role back (and privatize) Medicare and Medicaid. Now that the election is over it is time to end the rhetoric and place health care on a sustainable and available basis. This book offers a plan, starting with establishing health care as a right rather than a privilege. It would discontinue the existing government health care programs (Medicare, Medicaid, Veterans care), end the Payroll Tax and eliminate private health insurance. Medical care would be paid for by an integrated, universal; single-payer insurance program sponsored by the federal government...a revised, expanded Medicare. **The United States is the only major developed nation (Canada, Japan and Western Europe) that does not have government-sponsored universal healthcare.** This new Medicare insurance should cover: hospitalization; home care; long-term care; medical care - including reproductive services and preventive care, psychological, dental and lab fees; prescription drug costs; eye glasses, hearing aids; prostheses and other medical devices.

1) Vermont's single -payer system

Vermont last year became the first state to pass a single-payer health insurance plan. It may take five years to implement the plan under the federal health care reform law unless granted a waiver. Even though Vermont is a small state, the insurers don't want a single state to go single-payer. Last year single payer advocates fell just a few votes short of getting a a bill to the floor of the Senate in California.[83]

83 CommonDreams.org, *The Battle for Vermont's Single Payer System*

f. Funding/Cost

If Payroll Taxes are eliminated, how would I fund single-payer health insurance? This new Medicare would be paid for out of the general fund and I would raise Income Taxes as described above to cover the costs. In order to discourage unnecessary use of medical services, individuals would be responsible for a 20% copayment up to a total of 10% of their past years income. Children, having little or no income, would receive free medical care just as they get free primary and secondary public education, independent of parental income.

The cost of administering Medicare is currently in the 1.3-3 percent range, much less than the 12-14 percent range typical of big employer-based private plans, and the 25-30 percent overhead associated with individual plans.[84] Of course, profit must be added to these costs. Assuming continued administrative efficiency, placing everyone on Medicare would reduce the annual national health care costs by almost 2 percentage points (9% of current cost) from what it is now, roughly $190 billion. Additional savings in the cost of medical care is necessary to long-term fiscal control. This could start by negotiating the cost of prescription drugs with the pharmaceutical companies. An estimate of $50 billion per year can be saved here. Americans are the only ones paying so much for their drugs. Community clinics (already in process) could save a great deal of cost in emergency room care. The Institute for Medicine[85] estimated that as much as 30% of the cost of health care in the United States is due to inefficiency, waste (partially due to the lack of adequate and available records) and fraud. According to AARP Bulletin, November, 2012, the Centers for Medicare and Medicaid Services reported waste spending in health care in the United States amounts to **$765 billion annually**, broken down as follows: $210 billion – unnecessary services, $190 billion – insurance and bureaucratic cost, $130 billion – preventable errors/mistakes, $105 billion – excessive prices, $75

84 CommonDreams.org "Medicare for All: Fair, Frugal, and Inclusive" by Jonathan Ross

85 Ibid

billion – fraud, and $55 billion – missed prevention opportunities. This is unconscionable and must be corrected. We should take a hard look at the health care systems in other industrialized societies, all of which spend a smaller portion of their GDP for health care than the United States with better health care outcomes. Japan, for example, which spends one-half as much of its GDP for health care, has a universal system and apparently provides excellent care. Putting everyone on Medicare would eliminate the need for Medicaid, saving the states a great deal of money. It would eliminate the cost of private medical insurance paid for by business and individuals". Funding universal health care without tying it to jobs can increase labor flexibility and reduce the chance that people will fall into poverty because of medical emergencies."[86]

2) Social Security

"If you are not part of the solution, you are part of the problem."

Anonymous, Quoted by Eldridge Cleaver in a speech to the Barristers Club in San Francisco, CA in, 1968

[87]In the United States, Social Security refers to the Old Age, Survivors, and Disability Insurance (OAISDI) federal program. This program encompasses several social welfare and social insurance programs. The larger and better known programs under the Social Security Act and amendments are:

- Federal Old Age (Retirement), Survivors and Disability Insurance
- Temporary Assistance for Needy Families
- Health Insurance for the Aged and Disabled (Medicare)

86 Time Magazine, November 14, 2011, *What Happened to Upward Mobility?* by Rana Foroohar

87 Wikipedia, *Social Security (United States)*

- Grants to states for Medical Assistance Programs (Medicaid)
- State Children's Health Insurance Program (SCHIP)
- Supplementary Security Income (SSI)
- Patient Protection and Affordable Care Act

When most people talk about Social Security, Federal Old-Age (Retirement), Survivors and Disability Insurance is what they generally mean. When I discuss Social Security in this section this is what I shall be referring to. Other items in this list will be discussed elsewhere.

a) Funding

Social Security is primarily funded through dedicated payroll taxes called Federal Contributions Act tax (FICA). FICA imposes a withholding tax covering Social Security (Medicare is additional) of 6.2% of the gross earned income up to $113,750 per year (in 2013) on each of the employees and employers. For each calendar year for which the worker is assessed the FICA contribution, the Social Security Administration (SSA) credits those wages as that years covered wages. A self-employed person pays twice as much as an employee pays. However, if you are self-employed there are special tax credits you can take when you file your tax return. These credits lower overall rates.

b) Benefits

The largest outlay of OASDI is the payment of retirement benefits. A worker's retirement income benefit is based on his Primary Insurance amount (PIA). The PIA is the average of the highest 35 years of the worker's covered earnings. If the worker has fewer than 35 years of covered earnings, each year needed to reach 35 is assigned zero earnings. Years of work more than 2 years before the year the worker turns 62 are indexed upward to reflect the increase in national wages via the value of the average wage index (AWI). (Further details of determining the benefit can be found in the referenced Wikipedia article.)

The earliest age at which (reduced) benefits are payable is 62. A worker who starts benefits before normal retirement has his benefit reduced based on the number of months before normal retirement. Full retirement age (normal retirement) depends on a retiree's year of birth. It is now 66 for those born between 1943 and 1954. It will gradually increase to 67 for those born 1960 and later.

According to the AARP Bulletin, November 2012, "Over 56 million received Social Security [benefits] in 2012. Almost 25% of seniors rely on Social Security for 90% or more of family income. Do you how much they receive? Well, Motley Fool estimates that the average Social Security benefit amounts to only $1,177 per month. Factoring in Medicare payments that number drops down to $836 per month. Half of seniors have income under $20,000. They spend 17% of that on health care. Social Security is projected to pay full benefits until 2033, after that if Congress fails to act, there is enough funding to pay 75% of promised benefits for future retirees.

c) Disability Insurance

"The Social Security Disability Insurance (DI) program pays cash benefits to nonelderly adults (those younger than 66) who are judged to be unable to perform 'substantial' work because of a disability but who have worked in the past; the program also pays benefits to some of those adults' dependents. In 2011, the DI program provided benefits to 8 million disabled workers."[88] (Of course, disabled workers are not counted as "unemployed" in the official statistics.)

It seems logical that these benefits should not come out of money collected under FICA. Just another reason for funding Social Security by means of the General Fund.

---

88 *Policy Options for the Social Security Disability Insurance Program,* CBO, July 2012

d) Other Benefits

Other benefits include spousal benefits (in the event of divorce), widowed benefit (if a covered worker dies) and children's benefit (dependent or survivor). Again, the reader is referred to the referenced Wikipedia article for details.

e) Future Planning

A survey found that only 34% of younger people are confident that Social Security will exist for them." Is it time to permanently fix the Social Security system?

The majority of Americans think we need to preserve Social Security even if we have to fix the Social Security system. The suggestions on what to do are so variable. These include:

- Raise the retirement age
- Establish a needs test
- Remove the cap on payroll taxes
- Make all income taxable.

Not surprisingly I have my own views. The Social Security program does not contribute to the current fiscal deficit. However, if we fail to act, future benefits may be in doubt. It is my recommendation that as part of this fiscal plan we revise the way we pay for Social Security.

Under this plan, Social Security retirement benefits, now funded from Payroll Taxes, would also be paid for out of the General Fund. Funding Social Security and Medicare by means of the income tax would mean that all tax payers would contribute to these programs, and be eligible to benefit from them. (Since I am proposing that all income be taxed, high income individuals who collect Social Security would effectively receive smaller net payments. Those with incomes over $250,000 per year would receive no benefits. (See below.) Funding of Social Security would replace a regressive payroll tax with a progressive income tax. (Current Social Security taxes are limited to the first $113,700 of "earned" income, starting in 2013.) It would relieve business of its share of the payroll tax, thereby acting as a stimulant to business. Benefits would be based on an individual's lifetime income tax payments, with spousal and surviving children death benefits. Annual benefits might be set at 5% (with a realistic cost-of living adjustment) of total lifetime taxes paid, initially up to a maximum of $25,000 per year for retirement at age 67. Early retirement, at ages below 67, would be possible at a sacrifice of 10% of the full benefit for every year below 67. Retirement after the age of 67 would achieve the reverse, an increase of 10% for each year.

Despite the fact that Social Security does not contribute to the current deficit, this book recommends that it be funded in the future out of the General Fund, primarily through increased income taxes. Eliminating Payroll Taxes would immediately provide a significant increase in worker take-home pay and serve as a stimulus to the economy. It would benefit businesses by eliminating their share of the Payroll Tax making American business more competitive and motivating an increase in employment. Funding Social Security out of the General Fund would immediately reduce the federal debt by about $2.5 trillion (eliminating the Trust Fund debt), thus making the debt ceiling issue mute. So, while Social Security is not part of the problem, it can be a significant part of the solution.

Recently, a new approach to adjusting Social Security for inflation has been proposed by some, the so-called "chained CPI". This approach assumes that if the price of one commodity in the market basket goes up consumers will switch to a lower cost alternative. The net result of this will be a lower cost of living adjustment. On the face of it this seems reasonable, however, the selection of the market basket is intended to provide a balance taking such changes in to account. While the difference seems trivial (it would have changed the 2013 adjustment by 0.3%) it becomes significant as the adjustment compounds from year to year. Quite simply, this is an attack on the very concept of adjusting Social Security benefits for inflation.

What should constitute retirement? Today, one can nominally retire (collect Social Security) while continuing to work. I would propose that this be limited to lower income people, those whose income is below $150,000 (from all sources) per year. After that, recipients would sacrifice one percent in Social Security benefits for every additional one thousand dollars earned. Clearly, this would motivate higher earners to delay retirement. Some of these, whose incomes come from investment which continue independent of age, could in fact, never collect Social Security. They really don't need it.

There are those who claim the retirement age should be increased. The argument goes like this: since the establishment of Social Security the life expectancy has increased substantially. Thus, the initial retirement age should be pushed out. My reaction is as follows:

- The retirement age was set too old initially. Back in the 1930s very few people got to live much beyond 65 to enjoy their retirement benefits.
- The retirement age has already been pushed out by two years. It will soon be 67.
- Much of the increase in average longevity is attributed to the wealthy. The gain in longevity for working and middle-class has been considerably less. This is particularly true among those who do physically taxing work.
- Longevity is not necessarily correlated to the ability to continue working. While the elderly are surviving longer many are still frail and tired. Those who wish to continue working are encouraged to do so by this plan, since their benefits will continue to grow the longer they delay retirement.

3) Obligations

"The commitments we make to each other through Medicare, Medicaid and Social Security do not sap our initiative. They strengthen us."

President Obama's Second Inaugural Address

Medicare and Social Security are called "entitlements" because their funding does not have to be voted on each year. Some well-intentioned writers have started to refer to them as "earned benefits", because recipients have generally earned and paid for them. Unfortunately, for some, the name "entitlement" brings to mind people expecting a handout. I like the term entitlement, because I believe that is exactly what they should be. I think all Americans should be **entitled** to health care and old age financial security. I wish both of these programs to be treated as **commitments**, to be funded out of the General Fund rather than by means of payroll taxes. Some in government do not understand the concept of an entitlement and believe it can be reduced, modified or eliminated. Some have argued for privatizing Social Security and reducing benefits and/or privatizing Medicare. Funding Medicare and Social Security out of the General Fund would make them less vulnerable. (There would be nothing to privatize.) It would wipe out the so-called unfunded Social Security and Medicare obligations. Of course, payments would still have to be made, but they would be funded pay-as-you-go by income tax receipts, just as other government expenses are funded. (Many European governments use pay-as-you-go schemes, funding retirement benefits out of current taxes.[89])

F. Net-worth (Wealth) Tax

"Across America, the divide between the super-rich and everyone else has become a yawning chasm that studies indicate may stifle jobs and growth for years to come. At no time in modern history has the top one hundredth of one percent owned more of our wealth or paid so low a tax rate."

89 The Economist, 9/24/11 Buttonwood, *Pensions, Ponzis and Pyramids*

Bill Moyers, On Democracy, October 19, 2012

The separation between the extremely wealthy and the poor in America has reached a level where it endangers our fundamental democratic process. There are over 400 billionaires in the United States. As of 2007 the top 1% is reported to control 43% of the wealth while the bottom 80% has less than 7% of the wealth[90]. Since then the disparity has continued to increase. Sheila Blair, in an article in the NY Times, dated February 26, 2011, notes that, "Emmanuel Saez, a celebrated economist at the University of California, Berkley, issued a report on income inequality in the United States from 2009 to 2011, the first two years of the recovery. The richest 1 percent" he found, "saw their incomes grow, on average, by more than 11 percent. As for the other 99 percent, you guessed it, their income shrank by nearly one-half percent."

Over 50 million people live in poverty in the United States. OXFAM reports[91], "Over the last thirty years inequality has grown dramatically in many countries. In the US the share of national income going to the top 1% has doubled since 1980 from 10 to 20%. For the top 0.01% it has quadrupled to levels never before seen.

The political implications of this inequality are enormous. Sheldon Adelson is reported to have spent $150 million in the last election attempting to elect a Republican president and congress. While he failed to get the president he wanted, we shall never know how he may have affected the Congressional races. Surely, this type of mal-distribution of wealth cannot be good for democracy. It is completely contrary to the concept of one person one vote.

Beyond the political objections to extreme wealth there are the questions of fairness and of caring about our fellow citizens. What ever happened to compassion in America? George W. Bush was elected to the presidency as a compassionate Conservative. Are there any compassionate Conservatives left? The OXFAM report

---

90 Working Paper No. 589, The Levy Economic Institute of Bard College.

91 OXFAM Media Briefing, January, 2013

quoted above also lists the following issues with extreme wealth and inequality as follows: "1. economically inefficient, 2. politically corrosive, 3. socially divisive, 4. unethical, 5. not inevitable."

What is to be done about the divide between the super-rich and the rest of America? I propose a federal Net-worth (wealth) Tax. This tax would apply to all net assets owned by an individual including: cash, savings, personal and business property, investments, trusts, annuities, pensions, deferred income plans, etc.[92] Non-cash assets would be taxed at their then-current market valuation. The first $10 million of an individual's assets would be exempt, $20 million for property owned jointly by a couple. Thus, this tax would only affect the wealthiest 1%. The marginal tax rates proposed would start at 1% for those individuals with $10-20 million in assets, and increase one percentage point each time net worth doubled. The marginal rate would be 2% for net worth between $20 and 40 million, and so on up to a maximum marginal tax rate of 5% annually on net worth over $160 million. This tax would apply to all American citizens no matter where they live, as well as to all non-citizens resident in the US, and cover all assets whether domestic or international. Transfer of wealth overseas to avoid paying tax would be illegal. Already, in 2013 the U.S. with the help of Switzerland, France, Germany, Italy, Spain, Japan and the U.K. will impose bigger penalties for hiding cash offshore.[93]

I think that most people would agree that $10 million is enough wealth to assure a life-time of comfort...so this amount would be exempt from the wealth tax. The proposed tax rates start at the low rate of 1%, easily made up by income on the investment of this wealth. At this point it is more symbolic than significant. Few, if any, small business owners or farm owners would be affected. Only when an individual's net worth gets up to $20-30 million, or more, (paraphrasing former Senator Everett Dirksen) do the taxes received "amount to money". The

92 US personal assets are currently estimated to be worth over $40 trillion, excluding pensions. The largest categories include: Stock - $14 trillion, Residential property - $18 trillion. Pensions are estimated to be worth $10 trillion.

93 See reference 32 below.

Fed reported that household wealth in the United States is currently estimated to be $66 trillion. If 10% of this wealth were taxable under this plan, and if the average tax rate was only 2% it would bring in $132 billion a year. For the purpose of establishing a budget I have assumed $100 billion would be collected the first year.

A Net-worth Tax, combined with the Income Tax code proposed in this plan (eliminating all loop-holes and treating inheritances as taxable income), would have the effect of significantly reducing the wealth gap over time. This could have the very beneficial effect of reducing the impact money on our political system. (This would not replace a Constitutional amendment, or a new decision of the Supreme Court, stating that money is not speech and that corporations are not people.)

Of course, some may renounce their citizenship and relocate overseas to avoid paying taxes. This already takes place. According to a Bloomberg report, on April 30, 2012 Eduardo Saverin's name appeared on the U.S. Office of the Federal Register, which issues a quarterly list of people who have given up U.S. citizenship[94]. He is best known as a co-founder of Facebook, which went public in May, 2012, at which time he was said to make $3.84 billion. If Saverin did indeed give up his U.S. passport in order to avoid taxes on the money he brought in from the Facebook IPO, he'd be far from the first super-rich American to do so.[95] The number of wealthy Americans dropping their citizenship has grown sevenfold in the four years since a whistleblower at UBS prompted a crackdown on tax evasion, according to a separate Bloomberg report. It happens now, and could be expected to increase if this plan were implemented.

The difficulty in getting a net worth tax through Congress is increased because so many of the sitting Congressional Representatives are themselves wealthy. The net worth of the

94 http/Bloomberg.com/news/2012-05-11/facebook-co-founder-saverinigives-up-citizenship-before-ipo.html

95 According to an article by Roya Wolverson and Vivienne Walt, entitled *Take the Money and Run* in Time, dated July 30, 2012, 1,788 Americans gave up their citizenship in 2011.

wealthiest 80 Representatives as of 2009 was $291,093,347[96], an average of almost $4 million dollars each. It increased 41% from 2004 to 2009. (Mitch McConnell, Republican Senate Leader, saw his net worth increase from $3,072,514 in 2004 to $19,929,018 in 2009.) Today, it is likely to be even greater.

G. Estate Tax

Estate taxes are now set at 40% on estates worth more than $5.25 million (automatically adjusted for inflation)[97]. While this seems a reasonable rate there many ways of sheltering estates from being subject to this tax. Under this plan there would not be a separate Estate Tax. Inheritance over $1.28 million would be treated as income to the recipient without any further deductions or exclusions. Notice, it is the recipient, not the estate that is taxed. If, for example, the estate is left to a spouse and two children equally, the exclusion would be $1.28 million (the threshold for the maximum marginal tax) for each recipient, a total of $3.81 million. If the spouse were a joint tenant in the wealth, or a part thereof, half the value of the joint tenancy would be excluded. This provision, together with the Net-worth Tax would reduce the accumulation and transfer of great wealth from generation to generation. The impact of treating inheriting money over $1.28 million as income would only be felt by the wealthiest estates.

There is a movement today among many wealthy people to contribute at least 50% of their wealth to charity before they die. Andrew Carnegie was supposed to have said that no one should die wealthy. He was responsible for building many of the branch libraries in NY City and setting up the Carnegie Foundation. These contributions should be encouraged. but not by tax deductions.

---

96 Government Gone Wild Website, September 18, 2012

97 *Is the Estate Tax Doomed?* NY Times, The Opinionator, March 25, 2013

H. Tax Havens

In a recent article, the Economist suggests,[98] "If a tax haven is defined as a place that tries to attract non-resident funds by offering light regulation, taxation and secrecy, there are 50 - 60 such havens." The Economist goes on to say, "Nobody really knows how much money is stashed away: estimates vary from way below to way above $20 trillion."

How much is deposited by American citizens or U.S. residents is unknown. Under this plan all income and wealth would have to be divulged, and none would be exempt. This would be true for individuals, corporations and financial institutions.

Certainly, some would continue to seek gimmicks to avoid paying taxes. The United States would have to join with others to be sure that the true beneficial owners of this wealth and income are identified and that income on such deposits is reported. This would also help in eliminating illegal money laundering. OECD countries have already started to cooperate to crackdown on tax evasion. According to the Economist, "when the global financial crisis struck, many havens were put on the black lists. But despite the change in sentiment, few have disappeared."

The proposal offered in this book to reduce (or even eliminate) corporate taxes should mitigate to the desire by corporations to hide income in tax havens and encourage repatriation of profit to the United States. According to the Economist, "America could do more to reduce companies' use of havens, over and above cutting its own corporate tax rate. A proposal now on the table that would require American-managed-or-controlled firms to be taxed as domestic entities, even if domiciled elsewhere, would reverse the long-term expansion of tax deferral for offshore income, making profit shifting less attractive." This would be accomplished by the proposals in this book.

98 The Economist, February, 16, 2013, *Offshore Finance*

H. Outlays

In addition to increasing revenues, some federal outlays should be reduced. Savings should include the following:

a) Eliminating corporate welfare including fossil fuel and agricultural subsidies. Senator Bernie Sanders introduced legislation May 3, 2012 to end billions of dollars in oil, coal and gas subsidies. "The measure would do away with tax breaks, financial assistance, royalty relief, and many loopholes that benefit the fossil fuel industry. Under current law", he said, "more than $113 billion in federal subsidies would go to oil, coal and gas industries in the coming decade."

b) Reducing the number of Federal non-uniformed employees by an average of 10%. This should not be an across the board reduction. Health, Human Services and Financial Regulation - e.g. the SEC - should be exempt; while the Department of Defense administrative and subcontractor personnel should be reduced by at least 20 %. (Our active involvement in Iraq is over, with Afghanistan to follow.) In the past ten years, while private employment increased only 1%, government employment increased by 10%.[99] This trend needs to be reversed.

c) Medicare expenses should be reduced by negotiating the cost of prescription drugs, increasing efficiency and reducing fraud in health care delivery.

d) The Federal government could save as much $13.7 billion annually if it were to legalize marijuana, according to a paper by Harvard economist Jeffrey Miron. More than half of the savings, $7.7 billion, would come from not having to enforce the current prohibitions against the drug, while an additional $6 billion per year would come from taxing marijuana at rates similar to tobacco and alcohol.

Despite these potential savings, this plan calls for increasing the share of GDP spent by the federal government. However, three-quarters of the outlays involve Medicare (single-payer, redesigned to include Medicaid, veterans care and other previous government medical outlays) and Social Security. These mandated insurance expenses will be paid for out of income taxes. The increase in government insurance

99 Government gone wild Website, September 18, 20012

outlays in its share of GDP merely replaces the current outlays of private insurance companies for health care and that of the states for Medicaid. (Insurance companies now contribute a significant portion of the GDP in health care payments and hardly anyone blinks). Except for these entitlement outlays the government share of GDP will be about 7%. Of this, almost one-half pays for national defense. The remainder pays for all other government operations. This hardly seems to be an excessive share of the nation's GDP.

e) We live in a dangerous world. Though Americans are weary of war, they generally recognize that continuing threats require a strong military. Under the terms of the Budget Control Act passed last year the administration has agreed to reduce the Pentagon's budget by $487 billion over the next ten years.[100] These cuts should come out of cuts in non-uniformed defense department employees, contractor costs and the release of the reserve troops back to civilian life. No cuts in the regular uniformed forces should be contemplated. An additional $40 billion per year can be cut out of the Defense Department budget due to the assumption of health care for military retirees and military dependents under the expanded Medicare (single-payer) program as proposed.

Almost every federal agency routinely passes a yearly financial audit, except the Defense Department. President Obama should insist on an audit. There is probably no other department of the government in which waste, fraud and inefficiency are more rampant. (Not surprising, with the largest budget, but still, disproportionately large.) The procurement of new weapon systems needs to be reviewed in the light of current threat assessments, mission definition, cost escalation, program delays and alternative developments. For example, the F-35, which has seen repeated delays and cost over-runs, may have been overcome by the rapid evolution of unmanned drones.

Missile defense is probably necessary in the light of the growing world threat from North Korea, Iran, etc. However, there have always been serious doubts about the effectiveness of its elements. Before

---

100 The Economist, October 6, 2012.

deploying a defense system which could cost hundreds of billions of dollars, adequate testing and performance confirmation is required.

The United States spends almost 50% of the entire world's budget on defense. We simply cannot afford all of the new weapon systems the military desires. Careful choices and improved management are required if we are to maintain a deficit-free budget.

I. Budgeted Receipts and Outlays

The following chart summarizes the receipts of President Obama's 2013 budget proposal and that of this proposed plan:

Budget Proposals (Fiscal Year) - Receipts

Item Description Receipts	Obama's 2013 Budget $ Billions	Proposed 2015 Budget $ Billions
Income Tax	1,294	3,486*
Payroll Tax	990	0**
Corporate Tax/Fees	365	450***
Net-worth Tax	0	100
Estate/gift tax	12	0
Miscellaneous	301	227
Total Receipts	$2,902 Billion	$4,263 Billion

*Includes 50% of uncollected taxes (estimated to $385 billion in 2006. Reference: AARP Bulletin, March, 2012). A large part of these uncollected taxes are on profits on overseas deposits/investments by multi-millionaires. Treating inheritances as ordinary income, is estimated to bring in $150 billion per year based on a total net worth held by the wealthiest 25% to be $20 trillion, a death rate of 3% per year, and taxed at a marginal rate of 50%. This compares to the trivial estate/gift tax receipts anticipated under current law of only $12 billion. The remaining increase in receipts comes from treating realized capital gains as ordinary income, the elimination of deductions, and increased marginal rates for high incomes. Much of this increase for low and middle-income people is offset by the elimination of the individual contribution to the payroll tax, half of the total, ($445 billion) and private health insurance costs ($750 billion).

** These receipts will be made up by the increase in income taxes.

***Corporate taxes decreased, fees added

The following chart summarizes the outlays of President Obama's 2013 budget proposal and that of this proposed plan:

Budget Proposals (Fiscal Year) - Outlays

Item Description	Obama's 2013 Budget	Proposed Plan 2015
Outlay	$ Billion	$ Billion
Defense	700	593*
Other Discretionary	565	500
Social Security	820	820
Medicare	528	2,320**
Medicaid	283	0***
TARP	12	12
Full employment	0	100
Other Mandatory	571	50**
Net Interest	246	238
Joint Com. Enforcement	(71)	(71)
Off-budget Surplus	(38)	(38)
Total Outlay	$3,803 Billion	$4,633 Billion****
2013 Deficit	$901 Billion	0

* Assumes $40 million cut due to transfer of retiree and dependent health care to Medicare (single -payer), and reduction in non-uniformed employees.

101 President Obama's budget shows deficits continuing for the next ten years, with annual interest reaching almost $1 trillion by 2022.

**Covers the cost of single-payer health care insurance (expanded Medicare) for the entire population. The additional cost of Medicare is funded as follows: 1) Medicaid elimination, $283 billion. 2) Reduction in other government costs $594 billion. This number does not take into account $765 billion which could be saved by eliminating waste and fraud. 3) Increased income taxes on the middle class, $755 billion (fully offset by the elimination of 80% of current household medical cost, $400 billion, and the elimination of payroll taxes, $355 billion.) 4) Increased income taxes on high income individuals, (partially offset by other savings) $300 billion. 5) Previously uncollected income taxes through better enforcement, $150 billion.

***Mostly replaced by expanded Medicare and full-employment programs.

****Equal to receipts

Part 3. Jobs

"I don't want your millions mister,
I don't want your diamond rings,
All I want is the right to live mister,
Give me back my job again."
1930s song - lyrics by Jim Garland

We often hear that the unemployment rate in the U.S. has been dropping consistently [102]over the past two years. The official unemployment rate is now (as of February, 2013) 7.7%. As indicated earlier in this book that does not include those who have dropped out of the work force or have accepted lower paid jobs. While this is true, what is not discussed as openly is that the United States has lost almost 4 million jobs since 2007. In addition, over 5 million jobs needed to keep up with the growth of the potential work force were not gained. As a result the U.S. is currently short almost 9 million jobs. Do primarily to demographic change (aging/retirement) the share of the population in the work force (working or seeking jobs) has decreased from 66% to 63.5%[103] since 2007 so the impact has been less obvious. No fiscal plan can be complete without providing for significant job growth.

A. Full Employment

"Full employment is the most promising policy for fostering social and economic equality."

Robert Pollin, ***Back to Full Employment***

---

102 Economic Policy Institute

103 *Where Did Everyone Go?* The Economist, March 23, 2013

What is full employment? Robert Pollin examines this question in his book *Back to Full Employment.* "A workable definition of full employment" he states, "should refer to an abundance of decent jobs." It should include a "living wage." He refers to Lawrence Glickman's definition of a living wage as, "a wage level that offers workers the ability to support families, to maintain self-respect, and to have both the means and the leisure to participate in the civic life of the nation".[104] He references Michael Kolecki, that, "full employment can be beneficial to profits, because the economy will be operating with buoyant markets, at a high level of overall demand for products."

Full employment does not mean establishing some arbitrary percentage as an acceptable rate of unemployment. There will always be some who are unemployed. These include the "voluntary": the retired and those who chose not to be employed such as mothers of young children; the disabled: those who are unable to work; and what Pollin refers to as the frictional: those who are between jobs. There should be no one in the category of "involuntary".

The United States needs a strategy on jobs. Job loss in recent years has been due to a number of factors. These include:

- Off-shoring - particularly in manufacturing, but also in computer services. This has been due primarily due to low cost wages overseas and the availability of resources and skilled personnel.
- Increased productivity, which has permitted the production of required goods and services with fewer workers.
- Failure of the United States to provide incentives (taxes and otherwise) for domestic jobs. The result of the loss of production over-seas combined with the cost of energy import has resulted in a continuing imbalance of trade. As in the case of our debt, this cannot continue. Eventually, foreign nations holding our treasury bills will have to be paid.
- Loss of public employment due to state and municipal budget cuts.

---

104 *A Living Wage: American Workers and the Making of a Consumer Society,* by Lawrence Gitlin

B. Public Employment

"The government does create jobs, including teachers, police officers, firefighters, soldiers, sailors, astronauts, epidemiologists, antiterrorism agents, park rangers, diplomats, governors (Mr. Romney's old job) and Congressmen (like Paul Ryan). At last count, government at all levels — federal, state and local — employed 22 million Americans, with the largest segment working in public education."

NY Times Editorial, October 21, 2012

Binyamin Applebaum reports[105], "Federal, state and local government jobs now employ 500,000 fewer workers than they did on the eve of the recession of 2007, the longest and deepest decline in total government employment since the aftermath of World War II." While cutbacks in bloated government employment would be desirable if the right people were discharged, unfortunately, there is no way to assure this happening. Instead, workers have been laid off not based on performance, capability or even need, but too often on seniority.

Savings in outlays for states and municipalities resulting from federal funding of a single-payer health insurance will free up state and municipal Medicaid funds for increasing public employment in police, fire-fighting and education. This can make a significant dent in unemployment. There has been a large outcry against what the public views as government excess in pensions and health care for public employees. While some of this has been unfair, much of it is due to real concern. Too often, public employees used gimmicks to increase their pensions and/or retire early. These gimmicks need to be eliminated. Universal single-payer health insurance would eliminate much of the health care inequity, and income tax funded Social Security payments could help reduce retirement costs. This is largely up to the states and is beyond the scope of this book. However, that

105 *Austerity Kills Government Jobs as Cuts to Budgets Loom,* NY Times, February 26, 2013

portion of public employment which is federal should be addressed and equalized with private benefits and pensions.

C. Private Employment

Businesses increase employment in response to increased market demand and their need for personnel to handle this demand. Reducing the taxes and medical insurance costs for the working class will provide lower income people with increased purchasing power and thereby stimulate business expansion and employment. To further increase the working class purchasing power, and to help eliminate poverty among the working poor, the minimum wage should be increased to $10.55 per hour[106]. (This would bring the income of full-time employees above the poverty level. It would help 30 million Americans.)

Reducing corporate taxes, and eliminating employer purchased health insurance and payroll taxes will provide businesses with additional capital for expansion and improved profit. This, plus the incentive of further reduced corporate taxes for increasing domestic employment (see Corporate Tax), should stimulate the expansion of business and the growth of private industry domestic employment. Over the last few years, companies across various industries, including electronics, automotive and medical devices, have announced that they are bringing jobs home after decades of shipping them abroad. Lower energy costs in America, rising wages in developing countries like China and Brazil, quality control issues and the desire to keep the supply chain close to the gigantic American consumer base have all factored into these decisions.[107]

---

106 According to Ralph Nader, Common Dreams, June 15, 2012, this would bring it back (on an inflation adjusted basis) to where it was in 1968, improving the earned income for 30 million workers.

107 NY Times, *In Shift of Jobs, Apple Will Make Some Macs in U.S.* By Catherine Rampell and Nick Wingfield, December 6, 2012

D. Manufacturing

Manufacturing jobs, particularly labor intensive jobs, have been hit hard primarily due to outsourcing to lower labor cost countries. In all America has lost almost six million manufacturing jobs during the past 20 years (mostly in the last ten years), while the population has been increasing. Today, manufacturing employment is below 12 million. Historically, it was manufacturing that provided the opportunity for many families to work their way up the economic ladder. In the past, union contracts have too often made for inefficiency and been unrealistic in retirement cost. Tax policies have actually favored sending these jobs overseas. This policy must be reversed. Corporations should be given motivation to increase domestic employment.

China has been the largest beneficiary of the outsourcing of American manufacturing. This was primarily due to the low cost of labor in China. However, according to the Fiscal Times[108], "China's wages are rising by 15 to 20 percent a year...the Yuan is gaining in value. Reinvesting in the U.S. will accelerate as it becomes one of the cheapest locations for manufacturing in the developed world. Counting costs such as inventory, and shipping a Boston Consulting Group study maintains that in five years time the Chinese cost advantage could disappear entirely." U.S. manufacturing grew at an estimated 9.1 percent in 2010, with U.S. manufacturing having added 250,000 jobs in 2010.

Domestic manufacturing cost is actually already decreasing. Fuel cost has dropped significantly due to the availability if new oil and gas resources. Modernizing our power grid could further reduce the cost of energy. Eliminating payroll taxes for Medicare and employee medical insurance, as well as Social Security cost would make a big difference in the cost of manufacture in America..

The unions have become, of necessity, more realistic in job descriptions and benefits. The American automobile industry has seen

---

108 Fiscal Times, May 26, 2011, *Made in America: Manufacturing Jobs Are Coming Home,* Patrick Smith

significant gains since the bail-out of General Motors and the merger of Chrysler, not the least due to rewriting their union contracts. Ford now pays auto workers about $14/hour as compared to $24/hour five years ago. Now it is up to the government to eliminate tax loop-holes for overseas earnings and to reduce corporate taxes for increasing domestic employment (for my recommendations, see Corporate Taxes). The United States should insist on more realistic exchange rates so that it is less beneficial to produce goods overseas.

The Information Technology & Innovation Foundation (ITIF), in a study entitled *The Case for a National Manufacturing Strategy,* dated April, 2011, asks three questions:

- Does the United States need a healthy manufacturing sector?
- How healthy is U.S. manufacturing at the moment and for the foreseeable future?
- Does the United States need a national manufacturing strategy?

This book does not intend to review this report; it recommended that reader do so separately. But, its conclusions in broad terms are as follows:

- It will be difficult for the U.S. to balance its trade account without a healthy manufacturing sector.
- Manufacturing is a key driver of overall job growth and an important source of middle-class jobs for individuals of many skill levels.
- Manufacturing is vital to U.S. national security.
- Manufacturing is the principle source of R&D and innovation activity.
- The manufacturing and service sector are inseparable."

The writer agrees that a manufacturing strategy is needed. This strategy must be related to the long-term fiscal plan as it "relates to the nation's tax structure, regulatory policies, [education] and innovation policy." The plan presented in this book proposes a tax policy which would be part of an overall manufacturing strategy. The other items are better discussed separately.

A number of companies have already started to bring home manufacturing. The Economist reports[109]," GE has returned the production of fridges, washing machines and heaters from China back to Kentucky. Having shipped a great deal of its IT work outside America, the conglomerate is now shifting it back and taking on hundreds of IT engineers at a new center in Michigan." And GE is not unique. "The pull of low-wage countries is weakening. In a survey of big American Manufacturers by the Boston Consulting Group last spring, nearly two-fifths of firms said they were either planning to move, or thinking about moving production facilities from China back home."

E. A Green Agenda

Michael Pollin in his book, *Back to Full Employment*,[110] tells us, "The key finding of my research is that there does not have to be any trade off at all between jobs and the environment." It seems logical that investing in clean energy, smart grids, and public transportation will provide jobs. In the past the issue has been how to pay for these. This book provides the way to generate additional revenue that will permit government at the federal, state and local level to fund these, and other, green jobs.

F. On-shoring

The timing may be right for encouraging business to bring back work to the U.S. previously off-shored. Off-shoring was a product of several factors as follows:

- Low labor costs overseas as compared to domestic labor cost
- Availability of skilled labor

---

109 The Economist, January 19th, 2013, *Welcome* Home

110 IBID

- High value of the dollar in comparison to foreign currency
- Low transportation cost
- High energy cost in the U.S.
- Corporate tax policy which encouraged overseas manufacturing
- Proximity to resources
- Proximity to foreign markets

The last two of these are the fundamental to production and marketing. These will always serve to attract a certain amount of manufacturing overseas. The others, while real, are more transient. For example, the biggest beneficiary of off-shoring for manufacturing during the past decade has been China. But wages in China have been increasing steadily and the exchange rate has dropped considerably. Thus, the cost of labor in China has been rapidly approaching that of the United States. While there are other countries with lower labor rates, the pool of skilled labor and the availability of resource are much more limited. Meanwhile the ability to automate has reduced the portion of production cost associated with labor. The discovery of huge sources of gas and oil in the U.S. will likely bring down the cost of energy domestically, while it continues to increase overseas. Firms have begun to recognize the advantage of co-locating R&D with manufacturing. The proximity to the market in the U.S. with reduced transportation cost and time it takes to get goods to market motivate domestic manufacture. At the same time the reduction of labor cost in the U.S. (e.g. automobile manufacture) has made a significant difference in domestic manufacturing cost.

Indications are that many large firms are already beginning to bring home manufacturing. Reducing corporate taxes, particularly for increasing domestic employment as proposed in this book, as well elimination of deductions for overseas production should serve as additional motivation for continuing this trend.

G. Wages

For many reasons, wages for American workers have decreased in real terms for over ten years. Included in these reasons are: outsourcing, productivity increases (in many cases computers and automated equipment have replaced workers), the decreased role and effectiveness of unions. According to the NY Times[111], quoting the Center for Budget and Policy Priorities, "Median income for working age households (headed by someone under 65) slid 12.4 percent from 2000 to 2011, to $55,640, while productivity has increased more than 18 percent. (Note: this is household income not individual income.) Even college graduates have been hit hard.

The NY Times reports[112], "Low-wage, temporary jobs have become so widespread that they threaten to become the norm... American employers have generally [been] lowering wages and cutting benefits, converting permanent employees into part-time and contingent workers, busting unions and subcontracting and outsourcing jobs."

While it is not likely that this trend will be reversed in the near future (although bringing jobs home from overseas could help), this book advocates at least six policies which could make a major change in this trend:

- Increase the minimum wage. This would particularly help the less skilled working class. I was pleased to hear the President advocate such an increase in his state-of-the-union address. He offered the figure of $9.00 per hour with adjustments in the future for inflation. I believe it should be set at $10.55 per hour, with inflation adjustments. This figure would bring the minimum wage to the level it would be at if we adjusted for inflation since the time it was first established. It is also compatible with the level a full time employee must earn to take a family of four out of poverty.

111 NY Times, January 12, 2013, *Our Economic Pickle*

112 NY Times, January 26, 2013, *The Rise of the Permanent Temp Economy*

"Labor laws, still leave out some groups. The Fair Labor Standards Act (FLSA) is still interpreted to exclude home care workers from both minimum wage and overtime protections...The FLSA also excludes agricultural workers[113]" This law and others needs to be modified to be more inclusive.

- Mandate equal pay for equal work. This has been an issue with woman for many years. Although pay equity is better than it has been in the past, in general women are still paid at a lower rate. The argument has been that men, as head of households, require higher salaries that woman, who are often seen as second income earners. If this ever was true, it certainly no longer is true for most women. Today, a household can just as frequently be headed by a woman as a man. In any case, it is unfair.

But, this issue is today also applicable to many men. Even in unionized organizations, new employees are being paid at much lower salary rates than long-term employees, although they do the same jobs. Colleges and universities have hired "adjuncts" in place of regular faculty members and pay them a fraction of their professorial staff. It has been the practice for many years to increase wages as a function of "seniority", rather than productivity or special ability. Unions have frequently fought for this provision. The detailed resolution of this requirement will take some working out, but the general idea seems both fair and reasonable.

- Increase the competition for workers. There has been a theory among many economists that there is a natural rate (from 4-5%) of unemployment "frictional" - moving between jobs). This may be convenient for business but if it exists I believe it is much lower.
- Eliminate payroll taxes and replace these taxes by increased income taxes. While this actually doesn't increase wages,

113 IBID

unless the employer shares his saving with the employees, it does have a significant effect on take-home pay.

- Institute universal single-payer health insurance. This too doesn't actually increase salaries, (again, unless employers share their saving in health insurance costs with their employees), but it does mean enormous savings in health care cost for most people.

In total, these changes could amount to a significant increase in disposable dollars available to working and middle class families.

G. Job Guarantee (JG)/Employer of Last Resort (ELR)114

While the reductions in business expenses, coupled with increased disposable income for the working class, should expand public and private domestic employment, these stimuli will still leave some people un-employed[115]. I believe that no adult in America willing and able to work should be without a job. It seems to me better to pay people for working than to pay them while unemployed. ("Nearly 1.7 million New York City residents were officially classified as poor [in 2011], or with an income of less than $18,530 for a family of three. Some 750,000 were subsisting on incomes of less than half the poverty level. The proportion receiving food stamps increased to 20.6 percent from 19.3. Among poor New Yorkers 16 and older, a third had worked full or part time within the preceding year".[116])

114 I will employ the name used for this program in the book *Modern Money Theory*, by L. Randall Wray

115 While NYC has recovered in many ways from the recession, the NY Times, June 20, 2012 reported, "More than half of all of African-Americans and other non-Hispanic blacks in the city who were old enough to work had no job at all this year, according to an analysis of employment data compiled by the Federal Labor Department. And, when black New Yorkers lose their jobs, they spend a full year, on average, trying to find new jobs."

116 New York Times, September, 20, 2012

For those people left unemployed, the government should be the employer of last resort. (We could use the WPA and CCC as models.) This would permit us to eliminate unemployment insurance and minimize welfare, thus reducing the culture of dependency. (The Welfare Reform Act of 1996 required those receiving welfare to find a job after two years on the welfare unless they had children less than 6 years of age. However, the shortage of good jobs has made this program punitive, basically eliminating welfare as an entitlement for many. While the program encourages states to provide jobs, it does not require it, and, it is administered differently in different states. The proposed program would have the federal government provide a full-time job paying the increased minimum wage for all those willing and able to work.) People could be given jobs repairing infrastructure, reforesting areas which have been logged and mined, installing solar panels, aiding educators and health care providers, cleaning up our rivers and landfills, demolishing decaying structures and establishing and working on urban farms. Within two years, 5 million people could be put to work.

Those who are qualified and wish to could participate in alternative programs such as: paid training for fields which require additional workers and advanced studies, or a "Self-employment Assistance Program", as exists in several states. For those who have had their work hours reduced, we could institute a "Work-share" program, as exists in Rhode Island and Germany, where the government makes up for some of their loss in pay. Government work programs would eliminate the motivation to have children or to break up families to collect welfare. Free child care centers would have to be provided for the pre-school children of these workers and for after-school supervision. (The Welfare Reform Act of 1996 does not provide for child care.) These centers should also be made available to low-income families at minimal cost so that when people find employment their children will be cared for. ("Even before the Great depression, U.S. families have struggled to afford adequate child care, especially in households where primary care givers work outside the home. People in countries like France and Demark may pay higher taxes, but they get much more for their money, especially in terms of family and child care. Generous social welfare policies enable European women to more easily strike the balance between home and work life, their children enjoy better health care outcomes and higher levels of educational achievement, and far fewer are forced to live in poverty."[117]

For those who are physically mentally or emotionally unable to work the government should provide disability payments.

This program would be paid for with revenue received from the net worth tax discussed above and savings in unemployment insurance and welfare.

The book Modern Money Theory[118] reminds us that, "During the Great Depression of the 1930s the United States adopted several jobs programs. These were part of a JG/ELR program. The New Deal jobs programs employed 13 million people, lasting eight years and spending $10.5 billion. It took a broken country and in many important respects helped not only to revive it, but to bring it into the twentieth century. The WPA built 650,000 miles of roads, 78,000 bridges, 125,000 civilian and military buildings, 700 miles of airport runways; it fed 900 million hot lunches to children, operated 1,500 nursery schools, gave concerts before 150 million people and produced 475,000 works of art. It transformed and modernized America." This could happen again under the proposed full employment ELR/JG program.

H. Impact on Business

While this book is concerned with fiscal planning it is not possible to ignore the impact such a plan might have on major segments of our society. Jobs provided by the government, serving as the employer of last resort, could, in some cases, overlap with jobs otherwise done by employees of commercial firms. Arrangements would have to be made with such firms and with unions, where they exist, if the government is to intervene in these areas. It is not the objective of this plan to introduce

117 *Lessons from Europe: Let's Do right by Our Children* - Newsroom: Bernie Sanders - US Senate

118 IBID

workers doing similar jobs under private employment contracts or to reduce the established arrangement between workers and employers. For example, this might be the case in infrastructure repair and construction. In such cases, it might be necessary for the government to put the work out for bid, (possibly with the participation of state or local authority) with the proviso that additional workers required would be paid at union scale as trainees, and that they be considered provisional members of the union, thereby permitting the unemployed, non-union labor to join the work force. In other cases the entire job might be done under a government agency, for example, work done in the national parks.

Raising the minimum wage is controversial. Business' first reaction is this will cost jobs. There is ample evidence that it has not cost jobs in those states (19) which have raised their minimum wage above the national level. Raising the wage throughout the United States is much less likely to cost jobs. Companies cannot relocate to another state to avoid raising the rate. This argument can only be resolved by doing it.

I realize this is more complex than I have outlined above, but my purpose is to recognize that a process must be established, not to delineate that process here. That process must be fair to all parties and efficient in the use of federal funds.

I. Labor Unions

1) Right-to-Work

Over the past few years there has been a class struggle in the United States which is particularly focused on a war between labor and capital. One of its chief manifestations has been the growth of anti-union legislation. The earliest of these was right-to-work legislation, which prevents unions from requiring workers to pay union dues in so-called union shop companies. More recently, there has been the questioning of public employee unions, their job security and retirement provisions. Right-to-work legislation helped to spark the movement of many industries away from the unionized states (generally, in the north) to those which were less hospitable to unions (generally, in the south). This movement which started with this migration of manufacturing within the US, next saw industry move to Mexico to take advantage of still cheaper labor, and more recently to China and other Asian nations. In all, the US has lost about 1/3 (six million) of its manufacturing jobs in the past twenty years.

The movement toward right-to-work legislation recently achieved a major success in Michigan. It is the 24th state to pass such legislation. Michigan was at one time considered the heartland of unions in the US, as the automobile factories became unionized. The recent negotiations between management and the unions, under the provisions of the "bail-out" of the big three automobile manufacturers, had already forced the unions to concede many of it former gains in the interests of maintaining manufacturing in the US. The affect of this latest legislation on the unions is yet to be realized.

2) Curbing Public Worker's Collective Bargaining Rights

In a number of states, the right of public worker's to bargain collectively has come under attack. Legislation has been proposed, and passed in some states, supposedly to help state government to control costs. Particularly, teachers and other school employees have come under attack in Tennessee, Indiana, Idaho, Texas and Ohio. Curbing collective bargaining would affect the number of employees retained, their compensations and retirement benefits. While this legislation will have a significant affect on the middle-class, it is beyond the scope of this book to discuss the benefits and the costs of such legislation.

3) Federal Legislation

Eventually, the federal government will be drawn into this fight. President Obama has already been quoted as opposing some of the needed legislation.

Part 4. Education

"A Gallup poll found that confidence in America's public schools was at an all-time low...Politicians lament the country's poor rankings in international tables, [American students rank 25th in the world in math and 17th in science] or urgent need to produce college graduates. Poor schools, increased student debt, higher tuition fees...are causing more angst than ever about education."

The Economist, October 6, 2012

A. Vouchers

Vouchers probably represent the biggest on-going issue between the right and the left in education. Those who like them argue for school "choice". It is difficult to be against the freedom to choose a child's school when I am in favor of individual freedom to choose in other areas. The problem is that the issue of choice gets entangled in the issue of church and state. I might favor vouchers if they only went to non-sectarian schools, but, that would never please those whose children go to religiously affiliated schools. The Economist, October 6, 2012 points out, "Candidate Romney would take $25 billion of federal money that is spent on special education and poor pupils and give it directly to parents as vouchers. The value of a federal voucher would probably be too small to pay for anything except a bit of tutoring, online courses and after-school programs, but they would be particularly useful to parents who live in state that already offer vouchers. And the scheme would also encourage states to try to expand voucher schemes." The catch is that the money is to be taken from special education and needy pupils. So I don't support this idea.

Charter schools, however, which remain within the public domain, offer "choice" without vouchers. These are a mixed bag. Some have proven to be effective in improving the quality of education. Others have failed. Adequately monitored, I believe charter schools can play a useful role in improving our schools, if only by example. They are a hot potato however, in that they allow the school systems to go around the unions. Overall, I think if charter schools are limited to a small fraction of the schools available they represent a worth-while addition to the school mix.

The bigger question is how do we improve the quality of our schools? Ultimately, this issue is beyond the scope of this book, although I will provide some thoughts below. Issues such as class size, the length of the school day and school year, standards, discipline, the role of testing in teacher evaluation, teacher training and compensation all remain to be resolved.

B. Government Role

"In America, education has long been viewed as the main instrument for achieving equality of opportunity."

Springing to Life, by William H. Schmidt and Nathan A. Burrows, American Educator, Spring 2013

What should the role of the federal government be, if any? President Obama has increased the money spent on higher education without much effect. Some argue, not without merit, that federal money, including student loans, merely allows colleges to raise their tuition fees. In general, schooling is the responsibility of the states in our system. Unfortunately, in too many cases the states have not dealt with failing schools. President Obama has initiated a program of competitive grants to reward those states that create the best educational reforms, called the "race to the top". This seems a useful way for the federal government to get involved. Of course, this is an issue of fiscal priorities, on how we allocate government outlays.

Inequalities in the school curricula from state-to-state have had a significant effect on student academic achievement. As a non-educator it seems to me that the efforts to establish "common core standards" can make a big difference. "Recognition of the inequalities and overall weakness of mathematics standards in the United States helped to motivate one of the most ambitious educational reform efforts in recent decades; the Common Core State Standards for Mathematics (CCSS-M). Common standards would move the United states closer to what exists in most other countries."[119]The federal government should motivate and support developing and adopting standards across the board.

There is another area which the federal government should participate, raising the quality of teacher preparation. One suggestion worth considering is creating a a national assessment of teacher readiness, similar to the bar exam for lawyers. This would not require the expenditure of very much money. It would however, involve enlisting all of the "stakeholders" in the education system and working closely with the state education authorities.

It was great to hear the President address revamping our educational system from high quality pre-school to a redesign of high schools. The objective is much desired, but like many of the President's plans this objective will need a great deal of effort to be fleshed out.

C. Preschool/Daycare

Many studies have shown that children who start their education and socialization at ages as early as three years of age do far better in school and ultimately in life. "Interacting with other children means learning how to wait, how to take turns, and how to listen.

---

119 *Springing to Life (How Greater Educational Equality Could Grow from the Common core Mathematics Standard,* by William H. Schmidt and Nathan A. Burroughs, American Educator, Spring, 2013.

Young children learn social skills when they interact with other children. These social skills are critical to a developing personality... There are other advantages to preschools – primarily, they are the foundations for academic learning. In preschool [a] child will listen to poetry and songs—building blocks needed to grasp phonics and reading skills when it is developmentally appropriate. The play that takes place with water, sand, and containers forms the foundation for understanding some basic math concepts. Matching, sequencing, one-to-one correspondence are all activities that are done over and over in preschool settings and help children get ready to learn academics. Watching other children pursue a challenging task is also helpful. The presence of other children and a wide variety of materials are two big reasons why a preschool is a good thing."[120]

State/federally sponsored preschool school should be tied into day care provided to children of parents receiving jobs under the proposed full-employment program. It should also be made available to low income families at little or no cost.

The NY Times reported on February 13, 2013 that, "In 1971, when he was a senator, [Walter] Mondale led the congressional drive to make quality preschool education available to every family in the United States that wanted it...The federal government would set standards and provide back-up services like meals, medical and dental services (See my discussion on single-payer medical insurance.) Tuition would depend on the family's ability to pay. Mondale's bill passed congress but was vetoed by Richard Nixon. And, President Obama is trying, against great odds, to do something for 4-year-olds."

The President's expressed interest in preschool is welcomed, however, his objective of starting at age four is too late. Preschool should start age three for those who wish to enroll their children. A child's brain is developing very rapidly at this age, and children are especially receptive at this age to learning skills which have been shown to correlate with success in later life.

---

120 *The Benefit of Preschool,* Family Education Website

D. K-12

Education is critical to a working democracy. It is also critical to our continued economic leadership in the world. Not too long ago America was at the forefront of educational achievement. Despite school desegregation, there is an enormous disparity in educational achievement based on racial and other factors. "Achievement disparities are often attributed to socioeconomic factors. According to 2009 data from the Census Bureau, of all children younger than 18 living in families, 15.5 million live in poverty, defined as a family of four with less than $21,947 per year. This includes 4.9 million, or about 10 percent, of non-Hispanic white children, and one in three black and Hispanic children, at 4 million and 5.6 million, respectively" (Annie E. Casey Foundation 2011). "According to a seminal study of language development in 1995, by age 3, children in poverty have smaller vocabularies and lower language skills than children from middle-income families. Research has also shown that dropout rates tend to be higher for children who live in poverty. According to the U.S. Department of Education's 2011 Condition of Education report, about 68 percent of 12th-graders in high-poverty schools graduated with a diploma in 2008, compared with 91 percent of 12th-graders in low-poverty schools. A recent study by the Annie E. Casey Foundation found that children who both live in poverty and read below grade level by 3rd grade are three times as likely to not graduate from high school as students who have never been poor."

Education and school funding policies can exacerbate these opportunity gaps. Analyses by The Education Trust, a Washington-based research and advocacy organization, and others have found that, "Students living in poverty and those who are members of racial minority groups are overwhelmingly concentrated in the lowest-achieving schools. For example, in California, black students are six times more likely than white students to attend one of the bottom third of schools in the state, and Latino and poor students are nearly four times as likely as white students to attend one of the worst-performing third of schools. Likewise, research has shown that good teaching matters (The Teaching Commission, 2004), and that poor and minority students tend to have less access to the most effective, experienced teachers with knowledge in their content field. One study of 46 industrialized countries found the United States ranked 42nd in providing equitable distribution of teachers to different groups of students. For example, while 68 percent of upper-income 8th graders in the U.S. study sample had math teachers deemed to be of high-quality that was true for only 53 percent of low-income students."[121]

Scores from the 2009 Program for International Student Assessment show 15-year-old students in the U.S. performing about average in reading and science, and below average in math. Out of 34 countries, the U.S. ranked 14th in reading, 17th in science and 25th in math. Those scores are all higher than those from 2003 and 2006, but far behind the highest scoring countries, including South Korea, Finland and Singapore, Hong Kong and Shanghai in China and Canada."[122]

One has to be careful in comparing small, homogeneous countries with the US which is large and heterogeneous and has had such a large influx of immigrants. However, the fact is that America's youth must be prepared to compete with those of other nations. Based on test results, American students have fallen far behind. This plan will significantly reduce the number of children living in poverty, and, hence, improve the educational outcome for millions of children.

The elimination of Medicaid costs for the states and municipalities will free up money for investments in education. Some of this money should be spent in rehiring teachers and reducing class size. Teacher salaries should be increased for those with particular skills in math and science, and for those deemed outstanding teachers. This will require the development of approved evaluation modalities in cooperation with teacher unions. Details on methods, standards, teacher education, bilingual education, etc. will have to

121 Education Week Website, October 25, 2012

122 *Wake -up Call*, Christine Amarario, AP, December, 2010

be worked out with educators, but improvement in the quality of our education is essential.

E. College

"A college education isn't just a private investment. It's also a public good. This nation can't be competitive globally, nor can we have a vibrant and responsible democracy, without a large number of well-educated people."
Robert Reich

Between 1995 and 2008 the United States slipped from ranking second in college graduation rates to 13th, according to the Organization for Economic Co-operation and Development, the Paris-based organization that develops and administers the PISA exam. Of 34 OECD countries, only 8 have a lower high school graduation rate. College costs have also become a major problem. For the 2010–11 academic year, annual current dollar prices for undergraduate tuition, room, and board were estimated to be $13,600 at public institutions, $36,300 at private not-for-profit institutions, and $23,500 at private for-profit institutions.[123] Between 2001 and 2011, prices for undergraduate tuition, room, and board at public institutions rose 42 percent, and prices at private not-for-profit institutions rose 31 percent, after adjustment for inflation. Much of the cost of college education today is financed by student loans. The debt on such loans now exceeds credit card debt.

The cost of a college education must be brought within reach of all those who are qualified and wish to attend college. Two trends have been helpful and should be emphasized. The first is the growth of community colleges. Tuition cost at community colleges, are in the range of $2-3,000, far lower than at 4-year schools. Institutions should offer discounts to qualified, needy students. Arthur Hauptman writes in an essay published on Inside Higher Education, dated December 5, 2011, "We must also change the borrowing policy for

123 National Center for Education Statistics, 2012, *Digest of Education Statistics*

students taking remedial courses. Currently, because federal student grants do not cover the full cost of remedial coursework, most students who require remedial work are forced to borrow large sums to pay for courses that do not provide college credit. We should move instead to a performance-based system in which students would not be charged tuition for remedial course and the providers of remediation would be paid a fee by governments for doing so, with the providers who do the best job of increasing the competence of the students getting the most reimbursement and the most business." Hopefully, as the quality of the k-12 education improves, the need for remediation will decrease.

The second trend is the availability of on-line education. While such education will never replace traditional colleges, it can serve as a substitute for those who cannot afford traditional schooling. Municipal and state schools should offer degree-granting programs at minimal or no cost. There are already many sources of course material, both colleges and private organizations. These need to be integrated into academic programs leading both to liberal arts and science/technology degrees. Tied into municipal and state schools, they might require a short in-residence period at minimal cost before granting a degree.

Hauptman also writes, "Institutions [colleges and universities] must have skin in the game if we are to put a dent in the size of student debt. Currently, colleges can just maintain or raise their prices and shift the cost-sharing to loans for a broad range of students. This needs to change. One way to accomplish this would be to require that needy students not receive all of their aid in the form of loans. In effect, this would mean that institutions must offer discounts to needy students who borrow, thereby reducing their debts."

The details on improving the availability, quality, cost and financing of education is too broad a subject for in-depth coverage here. The point, however, is that the financial aspects of education need to be integrated into a comprehensive financial plan for

America. According to The Economist,[124] "The gap in test scores between rich and poor American children is roughly 30-40 percent wider than it was 25 years ago." This can be addressed in three ways: 1) provide universal, free preschool for all; 2) fix the public education system; 3) Eliminate poverty. All of these should be our objectives

124 *True Progressivism,*The economist, October 13, 2012

Part 5. Energy/Environment

A. Energy Independence

"The United States will become the world's largest oil producer by around 2020, temporarily overtaking Saudi Arabia, as new exploration technologies help find more resources", the International Energy Agency forecast in its World Energy Outlook The energy watchdog also predicted that greater oil and natural gas production - thanks partly to a boom in shale gas output - as well as more efficient use of energy will allow the U.S., which now imports some 20 percent of its energy needs, to become nearly self-sufficient around 2035. If oil coming from Canada and Mexico is included the U.S. could be totally free of dependence on sources outside of North America.

This assumes that objections raised by environmental groups do not prevent the U.S. from going forward using some controversial techniques, primarily hydro-fracking and tar-sand bitumen. There are realistic concerns about the effect of these techniques on the environment. There are also realistic economic and political requirements for the U. S. to become less dependent on middle-Eastern oil. These conflicting interests must be examined before a decision to bar or employ these techniques, and adequate safeguards must be provided in the event that the techniques are employed. It is counter-productive for green organizations to arbitrarily insist on baring these techniques.

1) Fracking

"Hydraulic fracturing is the propagation of fractures in a rock layer by pressurized fluid...Induced hydraulic fracturing or hydro-fracturing, commonly know as fracking, is a technique used to release petroleum, natural gas or other substances for extraction....Proponents of hydraulic fracturing point out the economic benefits from vast amounts of formerly inaccessible hydrocarbons the process can extract. Opponents point to potential environmental impacts, including contamination of ground water, risks to air quality, the migration of gases and hydraulic fracturing chemicals to the surface, surface contamination from spills and flow backs, and the health effects of these."[125]

Without cheap natural gas we increase our dependence on coal and foreign oil. "Fracking for natural gas is not the long-term solution we've all been waiting for, but it deserves to be seen as a critical transition fuel, one that will help us reduce our staggering reliance on coal as we usher in an ever-increasing use of renewable energy sources. Switching to sun, wind or hydro won't happen overnight and we should be receptive to a fuel that emits half the amount of carbon than the traditional electric generation of through coal. This strategy makes sense as long as it can be produced in a manner that protects out air and water."[126] Fracking must be regulated to protect our air and water. Under adequate regulation, fracking can be a significant contribution to making America energy independent.

2) Keystone XL Pipeline

Wikipedia says "the Keystone Pipeline System is a pipeline system to transport synthetic crude oil and diluted bitumen ('dilbit') from the Athabasca oil sands region of northeastern Alberta, Canada to multiple destinations in the United States...It consists of the operational 'Keystone Pipeline' and 'Keystone Cushing Extension',

125 *Hydraulic Fracturing*, Wikipedia

126 *Educate Yourself: The Pros and Cons of Fracking*, catylystnewspaper, December 14, 2012

and two proposed pipeline expansion segments, referred to as Keystone XL Pipeline and the Gulf Coast Project."

This pipeline would help to make the United States less dependent on mid-Eastern oil, and could reduce the cost crude oil and hence gasoline. It would also provide jobs to those constructing the pipeline and reduce the cost of domestic manufacturing encouraging companies to bring jobs home. "The Keystone XL Pipeline has faced law suits from oil refineries and criticism from environmentalists and some members of Congress." Wikipedia quotes a NY Times editorial as saying, "We have two main concerns: the risks of oil spills along the pipeline, which would traverse highly sensitive terrain, and the fact that the extraction of petroleum from the tar sands creates far more greenhouse emissions than conventional production does." On the other side, Wikipedia says, "In a speech to the Canadian Club in Toronto on September, 23, 2011, Joe Oliver, Canada's Minister of Natural Resources sharply criticized opponents of oil sands development and the pipeline, arguing as follows:

- The oil sands account for only 0.1% of global greenhouse emissions.
- Electricity plants powered by coal in the U.S. generate almost 40 times more greenhouse-gas emissions than Canada's oil sands.
- California bitumen is more green-house gas intensive than the oil sands.

These arguments are as yet to be resolved.

The Progressive Democrats of America announced a rally on February 17, 2013, in Washington, DC, "Demanding that President Obama reject the Keystone XL Pipeline project." This is an example of what I consider environmental extremism. Not that I favor the pipeline...but I do not believe we have sufficient information to oppose it categorically either. As I indicated above, in projects like this where America's economic interest may be in conflict with its environmental interests we should call for a delay while we carefully examine the considerations, set standards and develop specifications and then insist that any work that goes forward meets these requirements.

As to the environmental impact of the use of bitumen, it is not likely that this fuel will not be employed somewhere. Fareed Zakaria reports in an article[127] in Time Magazine dated March 18, 2013, "The U.S. Department of State released a report that concludes, 'oil derived from Canadian tar sands will be developed at about the same pace whether or not there is a pipeline to the U.S. Some will still come into the U.S. by train and some would be shipped to Asia". Zakaria also reports,' Opponents of Keystone say that the specifics are less important in this case and that it is the symbolism that matters...If we block this project - whose source is no worse than many others, rebuffing our closest trading partner and ally and spurning easily accessible energy in favor of Venezuelan or Saudi crude - it would be a symbol of how emotion has taken the place of analysis and ideology now trumps science on both sides of the environmental debate."

B. Smart Grid

The "grid" amounts to the networks that carry electricity from the plants where it is generated to consumers. The grid includes wires, substations, transformers, switches and much more[128]. A smart grid is an electrical grid that uses information and communications technology to gather and act on information, such as information about the behaviors of suppliers and consumers, in an automated fashion to improve the efficiency, reliability, economics, and sustainability of the production and distribution of electricity.

1) Smart power generation

Smart power generation is a concept of matching electricity production with demand using multiple identical generators which can start, stop and operate efficiently at chosen load, independently

127 *Build That Pipeline!* Fareed Zakaria, Time Magazine, March 18. 2013

128 Energy.gov

of the others, making them suitable for base load and peaking power generation. Matching supply and demand, called load balancing, is essential for a stable and reliable supply of electricity. Short-term deviations in the balance lead to frequency variations and a prolonged mismatch results in blackouts. Operators of power transmission systems are charged with the balancing task, matching the power output of all the generators to the load of their electrical grid. The load balancing task has become much more challenging as increasingly intermittent and variable generators such as wind turbines and solar cells are added to the grid, forcing other producers to adapt their output much more frequently than has been required in the past.

2) Sustainability

The improved flexibility of the smart grid permits greater penetration of highly variable renewable energy sources such as solar power and wind power, even without the addition of energy storage. Current network infrastructure is not built to allow for many distributed feed-in points, and typically even if some feed-in is allowed at the local (distribution) level, the transmission-level infrastructure cannot accommodate it. Rapid fluctuations in distributed generation, such as due to cloudy or gusty weather, present significant challenges to power engineers who need to ensure stable power levels through varying the output of the more controllable generators such as gas turbines and hydroelectric generators. Smart grid technology is a necessary condition for very large amounts of renewable electricity on the grid for this reason.[129]

C. Alternative Power Sources

"The Threat of climate disruption has become a dangerous reality. We cannot settle for half measures taken at a 'business as usual' pace."

Michael Brune, Executive Director of the Sierra Club

129 Wikipedia

There has been a great deal of research attesting to the fact the Earth is undergoing destructive climate change, at least partially due to the release of excessive amounts of CO2 and other "greenhouse" gases into the environment through the consumption of fossil fuels. The United States, as the largest per capita consumer of the energy among the great nations, must lead the way toward the efficient generation, distribution and use of renewable, clean energy.

This book would be incomplete without recognizing that a fiscal plan for America must include provision for investment in clean energy, both by private interests and by the government. Despite some false starts in this direction, the government must be involved due to the fact that near-term the heavy capital investment required will make the move toward renewable energy and energy efficiency difficult for private parties and firms to bear. Continued rebates for conversion to efficient products (cars, furnaces, lighting, etc.) will help. But, as indicated above, a major investment in a "smart grid" will be necessary to allow for distributed energy generation and transmission.

Crucial to the reduction of the release of CO2 into the atmosphere is the replacement of fossil fuels by "renewable' energy sources. The following is a list of the primary alternative energy sources currently under consideration. Each of these is not without its special problems, issues and costs):

- Nuclear power - Nuclear power is not truly "renewable", it consumes uranium in the process of generating energy, but is highly efficient. "One pound of nuclear fuel creates more energy than 830 barrels of oil, 240 tons of coal and five million cubic feet of natural gas."[130] Nuclear power is a problem: the cost may outweigh the benefits. Plants have been expensive to build and maintain, they represent a radiation hazard, and the disposal of waste has been a problem. Their big advantage is they generate no greenhouse gases.

130 http/cr.middlebury.edu/es/altenergylife/nuclear.htm

- Solar energy - "An enormous amount of solar radiation reaches the earth each year. In fact, if just a fraction of the sun's power could be captured and used as an energy source, the world's energy demands could be met."[131] Solar energy may be converted into electric energy by use of photovoltaic cells, or converted into heat. The disadvantages of solar energy are that it is only available when/where the sun shines and thus, large thermal masses or other storage is required, it occupies large areas, and at this point, it is expensive.
- Wind power - Ultimately, wind power comes from differential heating of the atmosphere by the sun and from the rotation of the earth. As such, it requires no fuel and releases no polluting gases. It does require large windmills and wind farms and has been found dangerous to bird life and an annoyance when built close to populated areas. Obviously, energy from the wind is only available when the wind blows and thus like solar energy requires large energy storage and back-up facilities.
- Biomass - In the form of wood, biomass, together with hydropower and coal, fueled the Industrial Revolution. In its simplest form it is used directly in combustion. In this manner, it still plays a major role in the generation of energy for use by mankind. Today, the term refers to all plant matter which may be used to generate energy. This is frequently accomplished by fermentation of starches and sugar to alcohol (ethanol). Since this process uses products such as wheat, corn, potatoes and sugar cane it is in competition with food production. It has the disadvantage of requiring a great deal of farm land, and there is some doubt as to just how advantageous the use of ethanol is in reducing the release of CO2 during its full production, refining and utilization.
- Hydropower - Other than human and animal power, this is the oldest source of energy used by mankind. Plants producing electricity from flowing water were widely

131 http/cr.middlebury.edu/es/altenergylife/solarpower.htm

constructed in the 1930s and are still widely in use. It is clean, cheap and non-polluting; however, dams constructed to support the generation of hydroelectricity have seriously reduced the supply of fish in some areas. Hydropower currently provides over 10% of the electricity in the U.S. and there are few additional sites left to be exploited.

All of the above sources of renewable energy are currently being explored. This book does not offer a recommendation as to which of these will be the source of the future. It does note that considerable study and investment will be required to replace the current fossil fuels. This will require significant investment by the federal government and industry. This plan will ultimately provide funds for this endeavor.

Part 6. Infrastructure

"Underinvestment in ports and inland waterways imperils American competitiveness."

Crying Out for Dollars, the Economist, February 2, 2013

The failure to invest in America's infrastructure has been widely decried. It is amazing that business interests have not been more vociferous in insisting that our bridges, roads, airports, rail lines, seaports and inland waterways receive immediate and significant attention. Even those who claim to be "self-made" must realize that without the ability to move resources and products American commerce will rapidly fall into decline. Still, business refuses to support taxation to pay for necessary repair and replacement. The article quoted above notes that the American Society of Civil Engineers (ASCE) estimates that "under investment in inland waterways cost American business $33 billion in 2010, and without significant investment those costs could rise to $49 billion (in constant dollars) by 2020." "The ASCE, estimates a five year funding shortfall for inland waterways - the primary mode of transport for much of America's exported commodities - [at] $20.5 billion." This is in addition to the dollars (many times this amount) needed to repair and replace our other decaying infrastructure, and to redo our electric grid to accommodate more efficient distribution of energy and new (wind, solar. etc.) methods of power generation to reduce global warming.

Much of this book has addressed the issue of social need and fairness. But, it also recognizes that business is the lifeblood of any society. The taxation plan proposed in this book will not only make for a more equitable society, it will provide the needed resources for stimulating business and for providing the infrastructure necessary to sustain commerce, society and ultimately, life. If for no other reason, business should support this plan.

When we talk of infrastructure we tend to think of transportation: roads, rails, bridges, airports, ports and rivers. But infrastructure covers a much wider rage of topics. These include: electricity, gas, water, food distribution; sanitation, garbage disposal, hospitals, communication, and school buildings. Many of these facilities are aging...in need of repair and/or replacement. We need an economic plan which provides the necessary financial support at the federal, state and local level that supports all of the infrastructure that makes our society work. I will not go into detail on each of these, but I will discuss a recent addition to this list -the internet - which has in a very short time assumed a critical role in our personal, social and business world and serves as a useful example.

A. The Internet

Today, the internet is a vital part of our nation's (and the world's) infrastructure, essential to the control and operation of virtually every aspect of our economy from government, industry and commerce to entertainment, education and communication. It also plays a vital role in our social lives. As essential infrastructure, it has become a public asset and should be considered a public utility. I define a public utility broadly. Something becomes a public utility when it becomes a necessity of life or necessary to the functioning of our economy or political democracy. If an item or service is essential to life it must be available to each and every citizen. This, of course, includes: water, food, energy (gas, electricity, petroleum products and other), sewage, access to communication, transportation, housing, clothing, medical care and a decent retirement. (I could add stable money, banking and finance.)

There are three ways to insure the availability of these necessities. The first is to have them provided by the government in the public interest. The second is to provide them commercially, but regulating them to assure that their delivery, availability and **cost** makes them universally available. The third is to assure a free market in the item. In America we utilize all three approaches, with more or less success. (Note: that I include health care in this list, an area where the private solution has failed to work, and where I recommend as a centerpiece of this book, a public/private solution...public insurance - universal Medicare - and private delivery - self-employed providers.) Unfortunately, with regard to the internet we have done none of these.

Electronic computers have made the internet possible. In the late 1960s and early 1970s, largely under the auspices of the federal government and a number of universities, a series of protocols were developed allowing point-to-point connections between computers. In 1982, the Internet protocol suite (TCP/IP) was standardized, and the concept of a world wide net of interconnected TCP/IP networks, called the Internet, was introduced.[132]

Connection to the Internet is generally provided through a commercial Internet Service (ISP) Provider. In many areas this is limited to one or two alternative companies due to the need for extensive (and expensive) interconnection most usually provided by microwave or fiber optics cable. The public has been poorly served by these limited sources. They have largely priced the poor out of the market and have been slow to improve the speed, quality and reliability of their products. The government should assure that cost-effective service is available to everyone in the market area, including individuals, schools, hospitals, and commercial users.

This topic is so broad and has so many possibilities that it can not be properly covered here. It has been included to serve as an example of infrastructure as "commons." The internet, as so much of our infrastructure, is a vital link among individuals on a national and international basis, and requires the protection of our nation, and other nations, to assure access to all. This will take a continuing investment and industry oversight. The interested reader can easily research the future of the internet using his/her ISP.

---

132 *The History of the Internet,* Wikipedia

Part 7. Effect on the States

While the federal budget under the current fiscal program shows on-going deficits the state budgets are under even greater duress. This is partially due to the fact that the state budgets, unlike the federal budget, must, by law, generally be balanced. (All kinds of gimmicks have been used to permit states to run a deficit while nominally balancing their budgets.) After all, the states cannot print money. As a result a great many public sector jobs have been shed. A large part of the decrease in jobs over the past three years has resulted from the states and municipalities cutting their payrolls to bring their budgets into balance. These cuts have fallen heavily on the uniform services and education "How many more jobs would we have if the public sector hadn't been shedding jobs for the last three years? The simplest answer is that the public sector has shed 627,000 jobs since June 2009. However, this raw job-loss figure understates the drag of public-sector employment relative to how the economy functions normally. Over this same period, the U.S. population grew by 6.9 million. In June 2009 there were 7.3 public-sector workers for every 100 people in the U.S.; to keep that ratio constant given population growth, the public sector should have added roughly 505,000 jobs in the last three years. This means that, relative to a much more economically relevant trend, the public sector is now down more than 1.1 million jobs. And even against this more-realistic trend, these public-sector losses are dominated by austerity at the state and local level, with federal employment contributing only around six percent of this entire gap."[133]

133 The Economic Policy Institute Blog, October, 2012

The states have been particularly heavily hit by the sequestration. An additional tens of thousands of jobs will be cut resulting from the cuts in funding in FY2013 in Human Services, Education and Labor, as well as many other miscellaneous areas.

New York State (for example) has been making a concerted effort under Governor Andrew Cuomo to balance its budget. Based on his Executive budget proposal, NY was expected to run a deficit of approximately $15.3 billion in 2012 out of a total budget of about $132 billion. Contributing to this deficit is a reduction in federal funding of approximately $5 billion. Among the major expenses experienced by the states is the cost of Medicaid. In NY State Medicaid was expected to cost the state $18.0 billion in 2012 and its municipalities $7.9 billion.

This proposed plan would transfer all Medicaid recipients into an expanded Medicare program to be funded by the federal government put of the general fund. This single action would wipe out the NY State (and many other state's) deficits as well as provide a great deal of assistance to the municipalities. This does not mean that the states should not continue their efforts to improve their operating efficiencies. But, it does offer the opportunity to stop the broad cuts in employment and to increase funding in certain critical areas such as the courts, education and infrastructure.

Part 8. Looking Back/ American Exceptionalism

"In its classic forms, American exceptionalism refers to the special character of the United States as a uniquely free nation based on democratic ideals and personal liberty"
Ian Tyrell

When Americans talk about "exceptionalism" we are thought to be chauvinists and distorted in our prospective. I believe America has indeed been exceptional and exceptionally fortunate. Great Britain was a harsh ruler in many ways, but, it also gave the colonists a set of institutions, laws and values which few other nations offered. Timing was in the colonist's favor. Great Britain was involved in a series of wars on the European continent which aided the revolutionaries. The Enlightenment and the Reformation brought about the stimulation of new ideas and the thirst for freedom. The Industrial Revolution brought technology which permitted rapid growth and expansion. The isolation of the Atlantic Ocean brought the colonists a great deal of freedom to govern themselves. It isolated us from a premature involvement in world affairs. Thus, when the nation was formed it had the benefits of English Law, and the experience of self-rule and a kind of sheltered environment.....and, a vast, temperate, fertile continent, replete with resources lay at our door-step.

The American Constitution gave birth to western democracy. With all of its limitations, (some of them have been corrected in the Bill of Rights - the first ten amendments, followed by the end of slavery and enfranchisement for blacks and women - it is still a work in progress) it established a form of government which has been the model and the envy of others for almost 250 years. A system of free enterprise brought the benefits of private ownership and equality of opportunity which drew immigrants from all over the world. The twentieth Century was unquestionably an American Century. From the building of the Panama Canal at the turn of the century, the United States emerged as a world power. This power was sometimes abused, but it was also used to intervene in two European wars (WWI and WWII) to defend democracy, to define a code of human rights and to establish international political and economic institutions. The end of the colonial era was at least due in part to American influence and ideals.

Sooner, or later, the world was due to catch up. Economically, the United States now finds itself in a world-wide competition. Politically, democracy has triumphed, although, not always with the American model. While on the whole this is very welcome, but it offers new challenges. The manner in which America faces these challenges will determine its role in the world during the 21st Century. America's most immediate, and crucial, crisis is economic – jobs, wealth inequality, poverty, affordable quality education, preserving and expanding the social safety net and reducing the national debt. Indeed, our system of democratic capitalism is at stake. Longer term, America and the world, face issues of living together in a world of growing expectations, competing ideologies, the threat of nuclear war, energy issues, global warming and shrinking resources.

Underlying American exceptionalism has been its openness to change. Whether on an individual basis, where neither social nor economic limits would stand in the way of the American dream, or national basis, where history was in conflict with ideals, did we not accept the status quo. The abolitionists would not accept compromise and the bloody Civil War ultimately became a war to free the slaves. And because the Black population would not accept second-class citizenship, we got civil rights legislation and school desegregation. The social safety net - Social Security, Medicare, Medicaid, unemployment insurance - was achieved over concerted resistance. Women's equality as citizen's, workers even as warriors meant the over turning of long held tradition. Change was won, not by compromise, but by standing up for what was right. In this regard, America has been a model for the rest of the world since its birth.

We still have work to be done. Poverty exists side-by-side with great wealth, racial prejudice has not been ended, anti-immigrant sentiment is widespread, and a no-nothing attitude toward global warming threatens our long term prosperity and even our way of life. Most immediately, an economic crisis must be dealt with. Once again, change must prevail. It will not come about through compromise but through commitment and steadfastness in the tradition of American exceptionalism.

Part 9. Middle Class

The American dream, one where everyone can aspire to riches, a dream of equal opportunity and upward mobility, has become the American myth. John Kennedy's vision of a "rising tide floats all boats" has become the reality of middle class immobility. And while middle-class incomes have been stagnant, upper-class incomes have skyrocketed. Although the current recession aggravated this situation the trend started long before the recession. Income for the middle-class has seen little inflation-adjusted increase in 30 years. Part of this is due to increasing productivity through computerization and the use of robotics, part is due to overseas industrial competition, both reducing the need for American semi-skilled workers. This is changing slowly as the standard of living and wages increase in places like China. Some say it is due to the influx of immigrants willing to take jobs at low salaries. This is doubtful. We have always had immigrants willing to take low paid jobs. This did not prevent the growth of the middle class in the years after the Second World War. The influx of women into the work force, who now make up almost 50% of the working population, and who receive less pay for the same work than men, is another factor.

A significant reduction in middle class income growth is also due to the decreasing role of unions. The fraction of union employment in private industry has fallen from 30% at its peak to 7% today. Much of this is due to the loss of industrial jobs, and the separation of the middle-class into two economic income groups. (See below).It is also partially due to the rejection of union objectives by the public and, even more important, it is due to the failure of government to support unions. (Legislation including "right to work laws" have encouraged companies to relocate and discouraged union organizers.) In the past year we have also seen an active effort to reduce the role of unions in government employment. Historically, unions have played an important role in the growth and financial well-being of the American middle class. Unless, and until, unions can find the means to organize our new service economy, it is likely that the middle class compensation will continue to shrink.

Each time an election comes about those seeking office pay a great deal of attention to the middle-class. Still, while they talk a lot about the middle-class, they offer few benefits to this group of voters. Sheila Bair writes,[134] "President Obama, who has rightly made income inequality a signature issue, cannot be pleased that the uber-rich have gained under the policies pursued by his administration, while the bottom 99 percent have not. Unfortunately, his team, populated by acolytes of the former Secretary Rubin, has relied on the same 'growth' policies that got us into trouble pre-crisis: generous treatment of the financial sector and easy money from the Federal Reserve. These strategies have done little to encourage sustainable growth, but they have worked wonders to increase Wall Street profits and inflate the value of stocks and bonds - which are disproportionately owned by the rich."

The agreement reached on January 1, 2013 delaying the sequestration was particularly punitive for the working and lower (see below) middle-classes. The deal allowed the two-percentage point payroll tax reduction to expire. While this reduction was not the best way to give lower income earners a tax break (It weakened the funding for Social Security) it was better than nothing. The impact is that someone earning $100,000 per year saw his or her taxes increase by $2,000 per year. It was also bad for the economy. The Economist[135] estimated that this expiration will reduce the purchasing power of workers by $115 billion, or roughly $1000 per household.

---

134 *Grand old Parity*, Sheila Blair, NY Times, February 26, 2013

135 *Nothing to be Proud of,* The Economist, January 5, 2013

In recent years the definition of middle-class has expanded to include families earning between $25,000 and $250,000. This encompasses about three-quarters of the electorate. I like to break this huge group into two groups. Those earning $25-125,000 I call lower middle class and those earning $125-250,000 (perhaps even $500,000) upper middle class. (A significant difference in those in the lower middle class from those in the upper middle class is the nature of their employment. Those in the lower middle class include industrial and construction workers, social service employees and government employees. Those in the upper middle class include: small business owners, information technology specialist, professionals, and middle management and mid-level financial employees. The lower-middle class, like the working class, is made up much more of people of color.)

The breakdown is convenient because the cap on income subject to Social Security taxes is $113,600 as of 2013. Thus the percentage of income paid in payroll (FICA) taxes for a single wage earner in the first category is significantly higher than that in the second category. This plan offers particular benefit to the lower middle class. By eliminating all FICA taxes a lower middle class a salaried wage earner can save up to 7.65% of his/her income – self-employed about 12%. Upper middle class wage earners will save proportionally less, but, still a significant amount. For many middle-class wage earners this will be the largest increase in take-home pay they have seen in years.

But that isn't all. By providing expanded Medicare to all Americans, this plan also adds an average of about $8,000 to each family's discretionary income due to the elimination of private health insurance premiums and the reduction of personal medical cost. Providing universal Medicare means improved health care of almost all Americans, and it has the additional benefit of giving a major boast to the purchasing power of the largest group of Americans, the middle-class. Thus, universal single-payer Medicare is the kind of economic stimulus that provides a double benefit. Who could ask for anything more?

Full employment will put middle-class and working class workers in a much more competitive position for jobs. This should inevitably work toward increasing salaries and benefits. While increasing the minimum wage is directly targeted to the working class, the increase in pay for lower-income employees will put pressure on higher-paid jobs, and should also result in middle class salary gains. Business will be able to afford these increases because of reduced corporate taxes, the elimination of payroll taxes and the savings in medical insurance costs for their employees. The increases in disposable income for the poor and the middle class should stimulate sales and increase profits.

Part 10. Housing

The Economist reports that, "The housing market has begun a long, slow process of recovery, but remains hobbled by many people who owe more than their homes are worth, by tougher underwriting standards and by the reluctance of private lenders to extend credit without a federal guarantee." That being the case Fannie Mae and Freddie Mac, which now back 90% of the new mortgages in any case, should become lenders of last resort. This would put pressure on the banks to resume lending. In addition, they should be prepared to subsidize the modification of mortgages which are in trouble. Fannie Mae should not be replaced as some have suggested, but it should be brought under much tighter control.

The elimination of the tax benefit for home ownership would certainly affect the attractiveness of home ownership. There is no reason to use public funds in this way to stimulate the housing market. If home owner ship is desirable on its own, it will prove attractive enough. There are many good reasons to own your own home rather than rent. But, the fundamental cost trade-off between the two alternatives should be allowed to work. In the free market prices would quickly settle out and stability would return.

Rana Foroohar reports, in her Article[136] in Time Magazine, dated March 18, 2013, "[The] housing market is back...new home sales jumped 15.6% in January...the number of private residential projects launched was up a stunning 82% annualized in the fourth quarter of last year." This is good news for the economy and for home owners. There are still many owners "under water" on their mortgages, but if this trend continues this problem should slowly work itself out.

---

136 *Why Markets Wont Crash -Yet,* Rana Foroohar, Time Magazine, March 18, 2013

Part 11. Looking Ahead

While I believe that the United States can succeed in balancing its budget without reducing social programs, I recognize that neither America nor the world can continue to consume on an ever-increasing basis. The American dream has been built on the view that economic success would be available to all, and, that our children will live better than ourselves. This has meant continued growth, without consideration as to what the Earth can sustain. Today, we are beginning to recognize that sustainable prosperity, rather than unlimited growth, has to be our future objective. Tim Jackson writes in his book, *Prosperity without Growth*, "It is now clear that the ecosystems that sustain our economies are collapsing under the impact of consumption…we will have to devise a path to prosperity that does not rely on continued growth." America, as the most prosperous large nation on earth, must lead in developing the means of production and manner of living that are energy efficient and habitat friendly. This could mean some sacrifice in our standard of living, but, if sacrifice is necessary, it must start from a more level playing field. This paper outlines a fiscal plan designed bring about equity to all Americans in 2015 and establishes a baseline from which we can build a secure future.

The government take-over of health insurance for all provides the opportunity to reduce the cost of medical care in America. If we can reduce cost by one-third, bringing cost more in line with that of the rest of the developed nations, we can save $850 billion per year. (Eliminating waste alone could result in a saving of $765 billion.) This saving, combined with increased revenue due to the expansion of business, jobs and incomes, could produce a surplus of almost $1 trillion. This surplus could then be used to reduce the national debt, improve our education system, expand employment, and provide the funds to invest in renewable energy, energy distribution and reduced energy consumption in transportation, manufacturing, heating and cooling. With these changes we will be well on our way to a sustainable future.

The fiscal 2012 budget provides very limited federal investment (less than $2 billion) in renewable energy, intelligent power grids and energy efficiency. It is worth noting that Obama did increase the fuel economy standards, a significant step toward more efficient use of fuel. The Whitehouse has issued a document, *A Blueprint for a Secure Energy Future,* March 11, 2011, which outlines its plan. That plan will remain a dream without significant funding for energy research and development and for a redesigned energy distribution grid. Under the existing Obama fiscal plan limited funding is envisioned for the foreseeable future...after all, the money just is not there. Under the plan proposed here, a significant budget surplus is envisioned as early as FY2016 as the cost of medical care is reduced, not by delayed or denied service, but by eliminating waste, fraud and inefficiency. The interaction of savings in one area making expenditures in another possible is an example of the integrated, systems approach to fiscal planning proposed by this book.

The housing market, already showing signs of recovery, should also respond to the general economic recovery. We can do more through Fanny Mae and Freddie Mac providing low interest refinancing to troubled homeowners. This too, should be part of the overall fiscal plan.

Part 12. Global Issues

A. Globalization

"Globalization [involves] the removal of barriers to free trade and the closer integration of national economies."
Joseph E. Stiglitz[137]

Stiglitz's definition of globalization is what we usually think of when the term is used. His book (referenced) describes, "the way globalization has been managed, including international trade agreements...and the policies that have imposed on developing countries in the process of globalization" We tend to think about Globalization's impact on our economic system, e.g. outsourcing and employment. Its impact is far broader. He discusses the International Monetary Fund (IMF), the World Trade Organization (WTO) and the World Bank and indicates that "every meeting is a scene of conflict and turmoil". This sad state of affairs, together with the international political issues (see below) has ramifications on America's (and the world's) economy, the federal budget and our overall well-being. Of interest are the conditions which globalization has imposed on America and the impact these have had on our economy including domestic employment, imports/exports and the balance of payments, military budget and international aid. I refer the reader to the referenced book for an excellent presentation of the economic issues involved.

---

137 *Globalization and its Discontents,* Joseph E. Stiglitz

B. Geopolitical Issues

I do wish to identify five issues which do not usually fall into the discussion of globalization and might not immediately seem to be related to America's fiscal situation. These are:

- Resource shortages
- Destruction of habitats and species
- The impact of global warming/climate change
- The effect of world-wide communications - the internet and telecommunications
- The complex inter-related areas of nationalism, religion ethnicity, war/peace and terrorism.

Each of these issues will require world-wide cooperation on a level not here-to-fore achieved. Each of these will call for policy decisions affecting the size of the federal government and the federal budget. Those who wish to shrink the size of the government and would establish an austerity budget which leaves little room to undertake the efforts required to address these issues are unrealistic and doing a disservice, not just to America, but to mankind.

Dealing with these issues is going be extremely difficult on a political level. But, ultimately, they will be addressed because the survival of the world as we know it is a stake. I will not attempt to discuss the resolution of these issues here. Such a discussion is clearly beyond the scope of this book. But I do wish to point out that the solution is going to involve dislocation, sacrifice and require a great deal of capital. Already storms, floods, droughts and forest fires have cost America billions of dollars. Things will get worse. America's fiscal planning must encompass the generation of public (and private) capital to lead in this effort. The plan offered in this book will do that as American industry recovers, unemployment decreases, federal receipts increase and waste in the health care system and government in general is achieved.

We must look to the future. It is not very far ahead.

Part 13. How Do We Get There?

I have any number of discussions with people about why we don't have some of the things recommended in this plan. The most obvious answers are the following:

- We have a divided Congress with significant resistance to increasing taxes and broadening social legislation
- Our President does not support the changes we want, or at least not with sufficient vigor to overcome Congressional resistance.

But, of course, we have this Congress because a large segment of the American electorate feels the same way. So it comes down to why does the electorate feel this way?

My discussions with others have usually come down to four issues:

1) Why are Americans so accepting of the status quo?

2) Why don't people vote their interests?

3) Why are there so many stupid Americans?

4) What are our responsibilities to our fellow Americans who are less able to care for themselves...the poor...the elderly...and the infirm?

Let me deal with these one at a time.

1) Many writers have asked this question in varying ways. Todd Gitlin, in his book, *Occupy Nation,* asks why "American's are so inert". We are not inert. There have been numerous movements outside of the main stream during our history. These either become co-opted

into the mainstream or just disappear. Examples which became absorbed were the Abolitionist movement and the anti-Viet Nam War movement. Examples of movements which have faded away are the Progressive movement and the recent Occupy movement. Even those that fade away leave some residue. Although our nation has been characterized by change, it comes slowly. We are, at our roots, a conservative nation. For many, the issue today seems to focus on the following question: Why do people vote against there own interests?

2) **People do vote against their interests as they see them.** Ultimately, voting for someone involves evaluation of the candidates as to leadership, character, capability, political affiliation and positions. It also frequently involves the candidate's ethnicity, race and religion. The candidates political positions may include: economic, social, religious and international views. Which of these areas dominates for a voter at any particular time depends on the voter's circumstances, beliefs, needs and prejudices. So it is not a question of voting one's interests. It is rather a question of making sure that the electorate gives priority to the issues we would like to move up on their priority list.

3) **American's are not stupid**. They are inadequately educated, under-informed by the media and poorly led. This is a huge issue. Improving the quality and availability of education and controlling cost has been much discussed. ("When all is said and done, a great deal is said and very little is done." - Anonymous) Let me just say here, that this is perhaps the most fundamental, challenging and long-term issue we face. It involves parents, children, educators (and their unions and schools), community and political leaders. It involves values, prejudices, and personal interests. The lack of quality education not only affects our political decisions, but is today jeopardizing employment and our leadership in the world both politically and economically.

Dealing with the media is another daunting challenge. Media today are increasingly part of large business conglomerates whose interest is primarily making a profit not informing the public. Accordingly, TV programs are designed to attract viewers, and newspapers and magazines to attract readers. This means that increasingly what passes for news is violence, sex and entertainment. Social networking has not improved the situation. It has shortened our attention span and distracted (particularly, our youth) from serious information exchange. The answer here can only be found in an educated public. How we get there is the subject of another book.

Finally, the election of our office holders is complicated by the lack of restraints on funding elections, lobbying and revolving door politics. Like our education system, this issue is much complex to address here. It would include: term limits, public funding, redistricting and party politics.

4) **Democracy, as we know it, can only survive if there is a sense of mutual responsibility among Americans**. Some have called this a "social contract". America has always prized individuality. This came about by the immigration of so many strong and independent individuals and was accentuated by the frontier mentality. We still talk about the "self-made" man, but of course, even self-made people had to stand on the shoulders of those who came before them... those who built our infrastructure, developed our institutions and legal systems...those who assured us of opportunity and freedom, those who defended those freedoms...those who worked in our fields, factories and mines.

Today, more than ever, we are mutually dependent. But, our willingness to accept our dependency is challenged by the increasing heterogeneity of our society. Increasingly, the poor and the needy of our society are people of color. Increasingly, we speak many languages and attend many religious institutions (or none at all). Many feel isolated and threatened by these differences, and are therefore unwilling to commit the necessary resources to public education and social welfare.

These issues are ultimately beyond the scope of this book, but it is clear that the plan laid out here will not go forward without facing them. Add to this the looming issues of over-population, climate change and world-wide culture clash and you have enough problems for the next generation...and then some.

Part 14. Conclusion

As I indicated at the start of this book, change has been inherent in America's development from its founding. If anything makes this nation special it is its ability to grow through change. Part of this is due to the foresight of the founders in structuring our Constitution, part due to our underlying ideology of freedom, and part due to the contribution of new ideas from the immigrants who have always flocked to this country. While change, like growth, is a continual process, the opportunity and need for significant change seems to occur each generation; driven by technology, demographics, culture, and external pressures. All of these conspire to drive our economic philosophy, development and change. Thus, the great changes associated with Presidents Theodore and Franklin Roosevelt, Johnson, and Reagan. We may approve or disapprove....but change will take place.

Once again, we find ourselves in a period of stress and self-evaluation. Our geopolitical dominance in the world is ending as other countries develop and join us on center stage. While the cold war is over, the threat from terrorism has multiplied. New, world-wide issues arise: civil strife, nuclear proliferation, global warming, resource depletion, habitat and species destruction and overall population growth. And, once again, this is a period of ferment....of opportunity, and need, for change.

Many of these topics are beyond the scope of this book. This book focuses on the American economic situation in general and its fiscal well-being in particular. But, economics is so fundamental to everything else that I believe the book is actually addressing our ability to deal with the broader range of problems.

Fundamental to our fiscal well-being are government revenues and outlays. People of all political and economic philosophies have addressed this problem. Some call for another fiscal stimulus, some for reduction in social welfare programs, and some for tax code revisions. Almost all call for tax simplification, usually as an argument for broader change in our tax codes.

There is little doubt that our tax codes have become encumbered with complexity and favoritism, resulting in waste, inequities, distortions and misplaced motivational provisions. When multi-millionaires pay proportionally less of their income in taxes than do middle-class workers, something is amiss. As this book makes clear, I am in favor of tax simplification. This should save individuals, most businesses and government a great deal of administrative cost.[138] I am also in favor of fairness. I believe all sources of income should be taxed equally, that itemized (non-business) deductions should be eliminated, and that the rich should pay a larger share of taxes. The plan offered in this book is comprehensive, integrated and fair. It provides stimulus to American businesses by reducing the cost of doing business, increasing profitability and providing investment capital. It motivates bringing home jobs from overseas. It increases the take-home income and reduces the taxes paid by low and middle income workers. Together with savings from ending the wars in Iraq and Afghanistan, eliminating less-needed programs, reducing the number of civilian government employees; eliminating corporate welfare and farm subsidies; reductions in medical cost and prudent cuts in other government outlays, (including the old standbys: waste, fraud and abuse); it is designed to provide sufficient revenue

---

138 "The most recent estimate of the current paperwork burden generated by the Treasury Department now totals 7.64 billion hours, according to data from the Office of Management and Ref: Budget (OMB). This massive time expenditure adds up to a whopping $227.1 billion, when calculated with the most recently reported average employer cost for civilian workers by the Bureau of Labor Statistics" of $29.72 per hour." A Taxing Trend: The Rise in Complexity, Forms, and Paperwork Burdens. NTU Policy Paper 128

to eliminate the deficit in FY 2015. It does this while extending Medicare to all and without endangering Social Security.

Extending Medicare to all will largely remove the insurance companies from health care delivery significantly reducing the cost of health care overall. Medicare will replace Medicaid and other mandated health programs. The plan also calls for an increased minimum wage and a full-employment program, with the government becoming the employer of last resort. This will virtually eliminate unemployment payments and welfare as we know it. These programs are intended to significantly improve health and reduce poverty in America.

I consider myself to be a fiscal conservative. (The term "conservative" as used by the political right, seems to mean anything but **one who wishes to conserve or preserve American values**. Mitt Romney has described himself as "an extreme conservative", (a contradiction of terms almost as misleading as G. W. Bush's "compassionate conservative".) I know some will laugh at the idea that I am a fiscal conservative...after all, this plan calls for eliminating all income tax deductions, taxing inheritance and capital gains as ordinary income, raising the marginal income tax rate and a new wealth tax. Add to that: single-payer Medicare for all, paying for Social Security out of the general fund, and raising the minimum hourly wage. My proposals are systemic (they work together), balanced and while fiscally "conservative", they are socially "liberal". Being a fiscal conservative is not the same as being a political (more often than not, social) conservative. Just look at this plan: it calls for balancing the budget, reducing corporate taxes, stimulating business by reducing corporate taxes, eliminating the costs for payroll taxes and health insurance for their employees and motivating private, domestic jobs. And, it calls for work to replace welfare. These are all **fiscal conservative** concepts. Yes, the role of government expands under this plan. But, shrinking the government is a political objective for some, not a fiscal concept.

Time Magazine writes, "The rise of the Tea Party and the weakening of the Obama economy have fueled a Republican narrative about "Big Government" as a threat to liberty, redistributing wealth from honorable Americans to undeserving moochers, from taxing 'makers' to freeloading 'takers'. Most Americans', Time continues, "are makers and takers – proud of our making and blind to our taking. Just about all Americans pay taxes: [income], payroll, state and local, gas and much more. The problem is that we pay in $2.5 trillion and pay out $3.8 trillion."[139] Making America fiscally sound is a fiscal conservative concept. This book proposes to do just that. Fiscal conservatism and political conservatism are often confused, even obfuscated, by some politicians. Congressman, and Republican candidate for Vice-president in 2012, Paul Ryan's "conservative" fiscal plan is not designed to "conserve"...it will destroy. It will destroy the middle class, Medicare and Social Security. It will exacerbate poverty. It will turn the American economy over to the bankers and multinational corporations. In an economy as large as ours, free enterprise requires big government to assure **democratic** capitalism...to minimize corporate dishonesty, exploitation, and financial manipulation; as well as to guard the public health, safety and "general welfare". In fact, there is no particular portion of the GDP which government should spend. It should rise or fall as needed and it has varied greatly in the past. While this paper advocates increasing the fraction of the GDP that the federal government will spend, **the increase lies completely in the area of expanding Medicare to replace private insurance by covering all Americans**. I too am concerned about abuse in the expenditure of money by the federal government, but Medicare has been among the most efficient federal programs. It has not been overgenerous to the health care providers (except the pharmaceutical companies due to Congressional restrictions) and it has kept overhead cost to a minimum. Waste and fraud have been extensive in the medical establishment[140], and that includes Medicaid and Medicare. After all, as Willie Sutton said about bank theft, "That's where the money is." With the expansion

139 *One Nation Subsidized,* Time Magazine, Sept. 17, 2012,

140 ibid

of Medicare, the medical establishment needs further regulation and closer surveillance to assure efficiency, control cost and prevent fraud. Improved oversight procedures should be included in the legislation which expands Medicare into a single-payer program for all.

Political conservatives criticize attempts at establishing an equitable tax code as the "redistribution of wealth". John Kennedy's aphorism "a rising tide lifts all boats" is associated with the idea that improvements in the general economy will benefit all participants in that economy[141]. That is sound **fiscal conservatism**. The Huffington Post reported[142], "Household incomes declined for the fourth straight year in 2011, the U.S. Census Bureau announced, in another reminder of the economy's failure to recover from the worst recession since the Great Depression. In its annual economic snapshot, the Census Bureau reported that "**the median household income—** half of Americans made more, half made less**—fell 1.5 percent to $50,054 last year**. Using inflation-adjusted dollar amounts, in real terms, incomes have fallen 8.1 percent since 2007, the year before the recent recession got started (it [supposedly] ended halfway through 2009)." In the past 30 years, income for top 1% has increased by 300%, while that of the middle class has stagnated. This is hardly the "lifting of all boats". This great a concentration of wealth cannot be fiscally conservative, a valid objective of democratic capitalism, nor is it a good thing for political democracy. Zanny Minton Beddos says," Growing inequality is one of the biggest social, economic and political challenges of our time." [143]This plan is designed to stop the **upward redistribution** of wealth. Justice Louis Brandies said, "We must make our choice. We may have democracy, or we may have wealth concentrated in the hands of a few, but we can't have both."

While equitable taxes are criticized, social programs are vilified. Unemployment insurance, caring for the poor, the sick, the disabled and the elderly are labeled "income transfer." (In reality, a great deal

---

141 Wikipedia

142 Huffington Post, Sept. 12, 2012

143 *For Richer, for Poorer,* Special Report, The Economist, October, 13, 2012

of the cost of these programs has been paid for during the working life of most people.) A government sponsored full employment program (despite the fact that it largely replaces welfare), undoubtedly will be called "socialism". The fact that other western democracies have far more comprehensive social safety nets than our own is considered alien and un-American. Senator Jim DeMint tells us in his book, *Saving Freedom, We Can Stop America's Slide Into Socialism,* "The nations of Western Europe capitulated to the siren song of socialism after World War II". European nations have not become socialist. (Even France, which has elected a "socialist" government is capitalist, i.e. the means of production is largely in private hands. It is more properly thought of as a social democracy.) The European nations have provided more comprehensive social services than the U.S. The recent financial problems in Europe are related primarily to public sector excesses in employment, compensation and retirement, inadequate tax receipts, and the recession/financial crises which have hit both the U.S. and Europe. Government funded health care programs in Europe cost far less as a percentage of GDP than our own public/ private programs and have better outcomes. (In America, the insurance companies have had their chance to deliver cost-effective health care. They have failed.) Perhaps the difference in attitude between the U.S. and Europe toward social programs may lay in Europe's homogeneity and America's heterogeneity...the fact that so many of our poor are people of color and that our immigrants have changed from European to Latino and Asian origins. Where this attitude exists it is bigoted and reactionary, and has nothing to do with fiscal conservatism. Heterogeneity has been one of America's strengths...immigration has been a source of vitality and growth... equality of opportunity is our mantra. We invented western style democracy and it has served us well. We should not forget that one of the stated purposes of our Constitution is "to provide for the general welfare".

Oliver Wendell Holmes said, "Taxes are the price of civilization. We need to be ready to pay this price by bearing a fair share of taxes…and remembering that compassion is the glue that holds society together". It is hard to see how in the present political climate we can fix our tax codes, with this, or any equitable tax plan. (How to fix our political system so that our government is once again, "of the people, by the people and for the people" is a subject for another book). Never-the-less, this should be our long-term objective. Thomas Friedman acknowledges former Treasury Secretary and Harvard University President Larry Summers as saying, "I think one has to be prepared to accept the long causal chains. That is, if you are trying to think about a problem and propose a solution, it does not happen the next day. But, it affects the climate of opinion, and things go from being inconceivable to being inevitable." Freidman adds (commenting about his own book), "If this book contributes in any way to making a real green revolution, spearheaded by America, I will consider it a success."[144] If this is good enough for Summers and Freidman it is good enough for me.

No country can continue to fund government operations indefinitely through the use of borrowed money. While deficit financing is a useful way of stimulating a lagging economy, or dealing with a national emergency, it should not continue to be used over an extended period. It has already gone on too long. Today, each American's share of the national debt is in excess of $50,000. Eventually, someone has to pay, and there is enough wealth in the United States to pay our way.

We have made great progress in this country in moving toward greater democracy. We have largely eliminated racial, religious and sex discrimination. We have a Black president and have had a Catholic one. We have had a Mormon and a woman come close to the presidency. We are increasingly represented in Congress by people of color and woman. It is primarily in making capitalism more democratic that we have lagged, and in paying for the government we want on an equitable basis. We are leaving our children a heavy enough legacy to deal with in the form of international conflict, resource exhaustion, environmental problems, energy issues, and food

---

144 *Hot, Flat and Crowded,* by Thomas Freidman

and water shortages. We should not complicate their lives through additional public debt, poverty and employment problems.

Abraham Lincoln told us "A house divided against itself cannot stand." Our democracy cannot endure 1% ultra-wealthy and remainder struggling to earn a living. Democracy depends on a willingness to share burdens. Extreme difference not only endangers the economy, but also jeopardizes political equality. This does not mean everyone must have an equal share of the wealth. It does mean that the wealthy should bear an equitable share of the cost of government. Why? Because they can best afford to without a change in their life-style and, because it will help to assure our democracy for all. The Supreme Court is wrong, money is not speech, but it certainly permits the wealthy to speak much more loudly then the rest. Franklin Roosevelt, in his Four Freedoms speech[145] said, "The basic things expected by the people of their political and economic systems are simple. They are: equality of opportunity for youth and for others, jobs for those who are able to work, security for those who need it, **the ending of special privilege for the few**, the preservation of civil liberties for all and the enjoyment of the fruits of scientific progress in a wider and constantly rising standard of living." This plan is consistent with these basics.

145 *A Documentary History of the United States*, by Richard Heffner

Part 15. Postscript

I am a realist. I recognize the difficulty of implementing the fiscal plan I am proposing in this book. But, that does not make me less enthusiastic to see these changes enacted. I believe the United States has come to a fork in the road. We must choose the direction we will take. One choice leads to stagnation and a loss of leadership in the world...the other a return to growth and constructive leadership. The choice is not between the present and the future. In his inaugural address, the President said, "we reject the belief that America must choose between caring for the generation that built this country and investing in the future." The choice is between oligarchy and equity.

The 20th Century was truly the American Century. America served as a beacon of freedom; prosperity; and industrial and military strength. Growth was the American mantra and "justice for all" the American creed. Sure, we fell short of our ideals, but the important thing was that we retained them. We talked of equality under the law, and of opportunity. Many of us lived this American Dream, and achieved the prosperity and the freedom our parents and grand-parents sought when they came to this country.

In a globalized world, our prosperity, achieved through political freedom, equal opportunity and democratic capitalism. is the model for billions of people. Many, throughout the world, are moving toward parity with us. It will not be possible to dominate the world economically or politically the way we did in the 20th Century and our planning must take this into account. As Thomas Friedman has said, "the world is flat." Never-the-less, many of the advantages the United States had historically still persist...our democracy, our vast temperate land, our natural resources, our know-how, our people (including those who immigrate here) and our peaceful neighbors. But, we must recognize that the world remains a dangerous place and we must keep our guard up.

While there are those who hate us, many more a trying to emulate us. Our military involvement in Afghanistan and Iraq is rapidly drawing down, and with this we regain the opportunity to look inward while striving to be a good neighbor. The motivation for cooperation is there. Trade plays an ever-increasing role in international relations, and, nations that trade are less likely to go to war. The threats of climate change, pollution and habitat destruction are global, and will require international cooperation if our civilization, and perhaps our species, is to survive.

Many of these subjects are beyond the scope of this book. But, all of them ultimately tie together by way of the economy. First, we must have a sound economy and full employment. A person who cannot feed his/her family has little concern about global warming. We need a strategy to make our country economically healthy and growing, one in which all can participate, one which will keep us at the forefront of international development and trade. The strategy we choose depends on our political and economic philosophy, and thus on our objectives, and an evaluation of the feasibility of achieving these objectives.

So, recognizing the limitations political polarization places on implementing a fiscal program like the one proposed, how should we proceed? Much of the answer lies in the commitment of the President to these objectives and his willingness to use his political capital to achieve these ends.

During his first four years as President, Barak Obama took the approach of trying to cooperate with those across the aisle. He showed a preference for compromise. The results achieved were minimal. The objective of the Congressional Republicans was to bring about his defeat, not to advance the economic interests of the country. Hopefully, President Obama has recognized that he will get cooperation neither from Senator Mitch McConnell and

Congressman John Boehner nor from their caucuses. The strategy outlined here is to fight them all the way, starting with the current "fiscal cliff" and debt ceiling, through the Congressional election of 2014. He must take his case to the people, ultimately asking them to elect a Congress which will agree on changes that benefit the nation as a whole. I believe this book has outlined such a program.

Appendix I

Recommended Reading List

1. *A Peoples Guide to the Federal Budget,* National Priorities Project
2. *The Little Book of Economics*, Greg Ip
3. *End This Depression Now,* Paul Krugman
4. *The Twilight of Common Dreams (Why America is Wracked by Culture Wars),* Todd Gitlin
5. *Back to Full Employment,* Robert Polin
6. *Beyond Outrage,* Robert B. Reich
7. *Plutocrats (The Rise of the New Global Super-rich and the Fall of Everyone Else),* Chrystia Freeland
8. *Modern Money Theory (A Primer on Macroeconomics for Sovereign Monetary Systems),* L. Randall Wray
9. *20:21 Vision (Twentieth-Century Lessons for the Twenty-first Century)*, Bill Emmont
10. *The Next Convergence (The Future of Economic Growth in a Multispeed World),* Michael Spence
11. *So Rich, So Poor (Why It's So Hard to End Poverty in America),* Peter Edelman
12. *Prosperity Without Growth (Economics for a Finite Planet),* Tim Jackson
13. *The Progress Paradox (How Life Gets Better While People Feel Worse),* Gregg Easterbrook
14. *The Price of Civilization (Reawakening American Virtue and Prosperity),* Jeffery D. Sachs

15. *Occupy Nation (The Roots, the Spirit, and the Promise of Occupy Wall Street,* Todd Gitlin
16. *Globalization and Its Discontents,* Joseph E. Stiglitz
17. A*merica's Competitiveness,* Economist March 16th, 2013
18. *That Used to be Us (How America Fell Behind in the World it Invented and How We Can Come Back),* Thomas L. Friedman and Michael Mandlebaum

www.ingramcontent.com/pod-product-compliance
Lightning Source LLC
Chambersburg PA
CBHW021347310526
45786CB00020B/491
9781481740609